Paul Gayler has worked in some of the most prestigious restaurants in London. He is currently Executive Chef at the Lanesborough Hotel, the UK's highest rated five-star hotel for cuisine. Paul is a member of the Guilde de Fromagers and the author of several books, including *Virtually Vegetarian* which was shortlisted for the André Simon award. This book is the first in a series, the second of which is *A Passion for Vegetables*.

Paul Gayler

A PASSION
for
CHEESE

More than 130 Innovative Ways
to Cook with Cheese

with photographs by Gus Filgate

KYLE CATHIE LIMITED

To my wife Anita and family,
with thanks for their continued support
and encouragement

This edition published in 1999

First published in Great Britain in 1997
by Kyle Cathie Limited
122 Arlington Road, London NW1 7HP
www.kylecathie.com

ISBN 1 85626 334 7

A Cataloguing in Publication record for this title is available from the British Library

Home economy by Louise Pickford, assisted by Zoë Sharp
Styling by Penny Markham
Book design by Kit Johnson
Typeset by Dorchester Typesetting, Dorset
Printed in Singapore by Tien Wah Press

The publishers wish to thank Michael Day of the Huge Cheese Company for his
donation of the cheeses used in the photographs, and the Guilde des Fromagers for
permission to reproduce their logo.

Photograph on page 2 shows Red Mullet on Baked Salad
Caprese with Basil & Olive Oil; photograph on page 6 shows
Lemon Blini with Ricotta & Raspberries.

CONTENTS

Foreword   7

Introduction   8

BASICS   16

FIRST COURSES   25

SOUPS   51

SALADS   67

PASTA, PIZZA, RICE & GNOCCHI   83

FISH, POULTRY, GAME & MEAT   101

VEGETABLE DISHES   131

COLD DESSERTS & WARM PUDDINGS   149

ALTERNATIVE CHEESEBOARD   183

Index   190

Acknowledgments   192

FOREWORD

In the UK 8kg (18lb) of cheese is eaten per annum per person. In France the quantity is nearly three times as much, at 22kg (48½lb). This disparity is revealing, and is not the result of French greed but of unfamiliarity, even fear, on the part of the British. Although many enjoy a decent cheeseboard, too few dare experiment with the more unusual cheeses on the market, and even fewer branch out when cooking with cheese. Parmesan and Cheddar may well be familiar to cooks, but who has the confidence to know what goes with Stinking Bishop, kasseri, Port Salut or Taleggio?

In *A Passion for Cheese*, Paul Gayler gives us the necessary confidence to try out his inspiring recipes. With the same skill as that of a professional golfer – imagination, patience, timing and conviction – he incorporates the cream of modern cuisine and the very best of international cheeses.

Paul has been cooking professionally for more than twenty-two years. In that time he has won the admiration of his contemporaries by his enviable knowledge, his use of unusual ingredients, his hard work and his impeccably run kitchen at The Lanesborough in London. His enthusiasm and integrity are as unforced as his cooking. As owner of the Huge Cheese Company, which supplies cheese to a great number of hotels and restaurants, I come into contact with many chefs and restaurateurs. In my opinion there are few chefs as accomplished in this country.

I met Paul fifteen years ago when he was competing for the Mouton Rothschild prize and was searching for a Mothe Saint Héray. No cheese wholesaler in Britain even admitted to the existence of this cheese, a full-flavoured *chèvre* from Poitevin, ripened between tree or vine leaves. Within two days I had tracked some down for him and Paul was cooking with it. He won first prize.

The French have honoured him both for his skill as a chef and his delight in and knowledge of cheese by electing him to the Guilde des Fromagers. As a frequent judge of cheeses at the Concours Général and as the UK's only *Prévot* of the Guilde des Fromagers, I have likewise been impressed, and sincerely believe our pleasure in food and in life will be enriched by reading and cooking from *A Passion for Cheese*.

MICHAEL DAY

Introduction

My intention in writing this book was to put together a collection of recipes that not only demonstrated the vast number of superb cheeses now available but also exploited their versatility and character. I didn't want to write a book about cheese itself since, after all, there are many writers better qualified than I am on that subject. I confess that when I was young I didn't even like cheese. In those days there was much less variety on offer and most of it was mass produced. But during my career I have been fortunate enough to travel and, as I sampled cheeses worldwide, my enthusiasm grew.

In 1987 I was one of six chefs from Britain to be awarded membership of the Guilde des Fromagers, an association founded by several luminaries of the cheese world, including Pierre Androuët, and dedicated to upholding traditional cheesemaking in France. I was consequently invited to join the Confrérie de Saint-Uguzon. At my initiation, an elaborate ceremony took place after dinner. A procession of *maître-fromagers* dressed in fur-lined 14th-century robes entered, carrying huge baskets that appeared to contain France's entire cheese repertoire. These turned out to be rare cheeses from small farms, and I can recall their wonderful flavours to this day, each one in peak condition. I'd never before seen cheese treated with such reverence.

It seems to me that the history of cheese cookery has been one of missed opportunity. In Britain cheese has mostly been banished to the cheeseboard, with a few much-abused exceptions such as Welsh rarebit and cauliflower cheese. The French have their classic cheese dishes, including soufflés and gratins, but they too tend to reserve it for the cheeseboard. Mediterranean countries are more comfortable using cheese in cooking, and the Italians in particular excel at desserts based on their delicious soft cheeses.

It is surprising that, to date, there hasn't been more effort to exploit cheese's unique characteristics in cooking. Why not pair blue cheese with white fish, or Cheddar with a lobster bisque? Use goat's cheese to make a pesto sauce? Add Sage Derby to a stuffing for quail? These are just some of the unlikely-sounding combinations in this book that have turned out to be real winners. But let's not forget old favourites either. Where would we be without Gruyère scattered over a vegetable gratin, the salty bite of feta in a Greek salad, and cool, creamy buffalo's milk mozzarella with tomatoes and basil?

A final word: although we are now fortunate enough to have access to cheeses from all over the world, I urge you always to buy local cheeses whenever you come across them. Better still, seek them out. Enjoy them on their own and then experiment with new dishes; you may discover your own great flavour combinations.

How Cheese is Made

Cheese could be described as an inspired collaboration between Man and Nature. Part of my fascination with it stems from the astonishing diversity that is created out of a single product – milk. Consider the sheer scope and variety of the world's cheeses. Then consider that they all are made from milk – many from cow's milk but some from the milk of goats, sheep, water buffalo and even, in some remote areas, donkeys and horses.

The magical property of milk that enables us to turn it into cheese is its ability to curdle. This is said to have been discovered accidentally by Arab nomads many centuries ago, when a bag of ewe's milk was cut open to reveal a curd-like substance. The heat from the sun had turned the milk sour, causing it to coagulate. Nowadays, most cheese is made from milk that has been pasteurized, that is heated to 72°C (162°F) for just 15 seconds and then cooled rapidly to 31°C (88°F). This destroys the bacteria that cause the milk to sour and curdle, so rennet has to be added to induce coagulation.

Pasteurization is a controversial subject, with many cheese connoisseurs believing that a great cheese can only be made from unpasteurized or 'raw' milk, since this contains the bacteria that contribute to the cheese's flavour and character. On the other hand, food technologists will argue that pasteurized milk is 'clean' milk. This may be the case in factory cheesemaking, where milk is collected in large tankers from a number of different suppliers, making it difficult to monitor the quality of the raw product. But farmhouse cheese is usually made from milk produced on the farm, giving the cheesemaker complete control over its quality.

The uniform character of pasteurized milk enables the cheesemaker to achieve a consistent product, which can reach a very high standard. But the truth is that the majority of great cheeses are made from unpasteurized milk, although there are some surprising exceptions to the rule, such as Colston Bassett Stilton.

Besides the type of milk used, many factors influence the character of each cheese, from the pasture, breed of animal, climate and even the time of year, to the way the curds are cut, the shaping, and the maturing process.

Once the milk has been soured, usually with a starter culture, rennet may be added and the milk clots into a fairly solid junket. This needs to be cut up to allow the whey to drain out. For softer cheeses, the curd is lightly cut and then left to drain naturally. For hard cheeses it is cut finely and then in some cases, such as for Parmesan, scalded, or 'cooked', at 41–54°C (105–130°F) so that it becomes dense and more whey can be drained off. The curd settles at the bottom of the vat, where it is milled again into small pieces.

Other than the softest cream and cottage cheeses, all cheeses are salted with either dry salt or brine. Some soft and semi-soft varieties are also sprayed and washed with various solutions or with bacteria. Such measures encourage certain styles of ripening and the formation of particular types of rind.

The curd is ladled into suitable moulds and pressed. Hard, compressed cheeses are pressed heavily, while the curd may be left to firm naturally or only lightly pressed for most soft and semi-soft ripened cheeses.

Unripened cheeses such as cottage cheese or fromage blanc are eaten fresh, but most cheeses go through a final stage of ripening, or maturing. This crucial process allows cheese to develop its character with time – from as little as four weeks for a Camembert to as much as four years for a Parmesan. During ripening, which takes place in a controlled atmosphere, the microbes and enzymes change their composition. Each stage contributes to the final character of the cheese and is carefully monitored by the cheesemaker.

Choosing and Storing Cheese

Always try to buy cheese from a specialist merchant, who will give good advice and, usually, allow you to sample what's on offer. Go for farmhouse cheeses, which tend to be far more interesting in character and flavour than plastic-wrapped, factory-produced ones. Whenever practical, purchase whole cheeses or blocks of a decent size. Small portions can lose their flavour quickly.

Advice on storing individual types of cheese is given below, but there are a few general guidelines to bear in mind:

The ideal storage place is a cool larder or cellar, about 10–15°C (50–60°F). This idyllic atmosphere neither retards the flavour nor hinders any ripening process. Nowadays, however, most people are resigned to storing cheese in the refrigerator. In this case, select the least cold part and aim for a temperature of 7–9°C (45–48°F).

If you do store cheese in the refrigerator, place each one in a separate airtight container. Certain varieties, notably the strong-smelling ones, are best wrapped in foil first. Avoid plastic film as it makes cheese sweat. Any cheese sold in its own box, Camembert for example, should be stored in the box. I never freeze cheese, as all too often this gives it a dry, grainy texture.

Hard and Semi-Hard Cheeses

Hard cheeses are ones that have been heavily pressed to give them a dense texture. The hardest include the extra-firm Italian *grana* cheeses, of which Parmigiano Reggiano, commonly known as Parmesan, is the most highly esteemed. Wonderful for grating, the *grana* cheeses also include grana padana and pecorino Romano, which is made from sheep's milk.

At the softer end of the range are the semi-hard cheeses, which include Tilsit, Danbo, Samsoe, Manchego, California's Monterey Jack, and Lancashire – of which the finest is probably Kirkham's Lancashire, one of my favourite cheeses.

Somewhere in the middle of the hard and semi-hard category is a huge grouping that includes three sub-groups: Cheddar-type cheeses, Gouda-type and Gruyère-type.

Cheddar-type cheeses are cooked, pressed cheeses of middling firmness. They are prized all over the world for their sweet, full flavour and culinary adaptability. Hence it is possible to find Cheddars of English, American, Canadian, Australian and New Zealand origin. France's equivalent is Cantal. However, the only true Cheddars are the great English farmhouse cheeses, such as Montgomery's and Keen's from Somerset and Gospel Green from Surrey. Other cheeses related to this family are crumbly, piquant Cheshire (I am particularly fond of Appleby's Cheshire); very crumbly, mild Caerphilly, of which the supreme example is Duckett's Caerphilly; mellow Double Gloucester, orange-hued Leicester and mottled-green Sage Derby, whose curds are infused with liquid sage extract.

Gouda-type cheeses are typically straw-coloured with a thin rind and a coating of paraffin wax. Although Holland's authentic Gouda continues to be made in the town of that name near Amsterdam, other countries produce versions of it under an assortment of names – Teifi (Welsh), Broodkaas (Belgian) and German Gouda. Similar to Gouda is Edam, which is made of partially skimmed milk and therefore popular with those who count calories.

Gruyère-type cheeses range in flavour from a mellow nuttiness to a rich, full taste that is almost fruity and sweet. Their characteristic holes are formed by adding the popolonic acid bacterium. Swiss Gruyère has tiny pinprick holes spaced so far apart that they are sometimes difficult to see. Comté, Appenzell and fontina have virtually no holes at all. The Norwegian cheese Jarlsberg has large holes, eclipsed only by the huge ones of Emmenthal.

Gruyère-type cheeses are invaluable in the kitchen. They grate cleanly and effortlessly, melt down rapidly and smoothly, and lend their fine, nutty flavour to a dish without overwhelming the other ingredients.

CHOOSING AND STORING
Even the hardest of the *grana* cheeses should be moist. The rind and surface should not be cracked, neither should the surface show signs of sweating. Avoid Cheddar-types that are darker near the rind or at their cut edges, as this may indicate that they have dried out. Never buy pre-grated *grana* cheeses, no matter how fresh they claim to be, the flavour will deteriorate within hours.

Grana cheese such as Parmesan that you intend to use for grating will keep very well double-wrapped in foil in the refrigerator. Hard and semi-hard cheeses for the cheeseboard should, ideally, be stored in a cool larder, with the cut surfaces covered by foil and the crust free to breathe. Failing that, store them as for *grana* cheeses for grating. They will keep well in the refrigerator for at least a week but no more than two. Bring them to room temperature before serving.

Soft and Semi-Soft Ripened Cheeses

These have a high water content and undergo a similar ripening process to the above. Soft ripened cheeses contain 50–70 per cent water, are spreadable and include Brie, Camembert, Bonchester and Pencarreg. Semi-soft ripened cheeses, such as Bel Paese, Gubbeen and Reblochon, contain 40–50 per cent water and often feel springy to the touch.

Because they are moist and therefore more susceptible to microbes than hard cheeses, they ripen in a matter of weeks rather than months. Unlike hard cheeses, which are ripened from within by adding a starter bacteria to them, soft ripened cheeses are ripened from the outside, by the action of a surface mould which is sprayed on after salting. In order to create a bloomy white rind, such as the one on Brie, Camembert and Coulommiers, the cheese is sprayed with the mould *Penicillium candidum*. The relatively mild, creamy characteristics of semi-soft cheeses such as Bel Paese and Morbier are achieved by washing the rind with a brine that slows down bacterial development.

Some semi-soft varieties, such as Port Salut, Münster and Reblochon, are known as monastery cheeses because they are ripened by a method developed by Trappist monks. The rind is washed with solutions that include alcohol – usually wine, beer or liqueur – resulting in a tangy flavour, savoury aroma and distinctive rind. Nowadays a culture of *Breyibacterium linens* might be used instead. This creates a thin, yellowish-red bacterial growth on the rind, which is not eaten.

CHOOSING AND STORING
Soft ripened cheeses with white bloomy rinds should never smell of ammonia, nor should their rind show signs of hardness or browning. The paste should not ooze excessively. Ripe, whole cheeses should feel springy to the touch. The paste of cut wedges should look plump and even textured; a chalky line indicates underripeness.

Semi-soft ripened cheeses, including the monastery varieties, should possess a fruity – but never rank – aroma and feel slightly elastic. The rind should look fresh and ungummy.

Store soft and semi-soft ripened cheeses wrapped – or in the case of monastery cheeses doubled-wrapped – in foil in an airtight box in the refrigerator. The soft cheese Vacherin Mont d'Or is a case apart: it should never be refrigerated. You should keep it in a cool, damp place and press a block of wood against cut surfaces to prevent them running.

Bring soft ripened varieties to room temperature for two hours before serving. Once fully ripe they stay at their best for only a day or two. Semi-soft ripened cheeses such as Bel Paese keep for up to ten days, while the monastery cheeses vary in their keeping ability – from two to three days for Pont l'Évêque and up to a week for Reblochon.

Soft Fresh Cheeses

These are uncooked and unripened cheeses. Uncooked means that the curds are not heated in their whey – which would encourage them to harden and cohere – while unripened indicates that the cheeses have not been ripened for more than a few days. They are too young to have developed any rind. Most soft fresh cheeses are made from cow's milk, often skimmed of its fat. Examples include cottage cheese, curd cheese, fromage frais, fromage blanc, quark and American pot cheese.

Fresh ricotta, one of the gems of Piedmont, is different. Traditionally it is prepared from the whey left over from sheep's milk after making pecorino. However, sometimes the whey from other cheeses, including cow's milk varieties, is used. Ricotta's dry, bland texture makes it ideal for blending with other ingredients in both savoury and sweet dishes.

Cream cheese is, as the name implies, made from cream rather than milk. One of the most celebrated examples is the devastatingly rich mascarpone, which was originally made only in Lombardy in autumn and winter. It is created from cream that has been skimmed from whole milk. Once its curds have formed, they are drained for about twenty-four hours and then whipped to a texture like very thick double cream. Mascarpone tastes delicate and slightly sweet and has a range of culinary uses, its affinity with fruit and chocolate being surpassed only by its empathy with savoury ingredients.

CHOOSING AND STORING

These cheeses should look and smell very fresh, clean and white, with no grubby edges. On no account should they ever taste bitter. Ricotta bought loose from a good Italian delicatessen or cheese shop has an incomparable sweet, fresh flavour that bears no resemblance to the type sold in tubs. It must be eaten within a day or two, though, as the flavour becomes tainted very quickly.

All soft fresh cheeses are highly perishable. If possible, use a cool bag to carry them home and then put them on the coldest shelf of the refrigerator. Very moist types of ricotta, cottage and curd cheese benefit from being stored in the refrigerator on a draining plate covered with a bowl. The drier fresh cheeses, including cream cheese, can be placed directly in an airtight container – lined with wax paper or foil if you wish. Use soft fresh cheese within four days.

Pasta Filata Cheeses

Pasta filata is an Italian term meaning 'spun paste' and refers to a technique of immersing the curd in hot water or whey, then kneading and stretching it. Well known pasta filata cheeses include mozzarella, a semi-soft, unripened cheese made with the milk of cows or water buffalo; provolone, a ripened cheese that is available as a mild dolce or a stronger-tasting piccante; and Caciocavello, which is also ripened, often smoked, and can be just firm enough to slice when young or hard enough to grate when mature. All such cheeses are widely used in the Italian kitchen, especially for toppings, fillings and stuffings.

CHOOSING AND STORING

If bought loose from an Italian grocer, mozzarella should have an immaculately white colour and a fresh, lactic smell. Otherwise, buy the type sold in a little sachet of whey rather than the dry, plastic-wrapped ones. Buffalo's milk mozzarella is considered superior to cow's milk because of its stronger flavour and softer, less rubbery texture. Provolone should possess a faint, lactic aroma. With both provolone and Caciocavello, look for a fine glossy rind and avoid holes in the paste, as these may indicate internal fermentation.

Mozzarella bought loose should immediately be immersed in milk, kept in the refrigerator and consumed within five days. With supermarket versions in their sealed bags of whey, honour the use-by date and keep any partially used portions in the whey in a dish. Store provolone and Caciocavello double-wrapped in foil. Provolone will keep well for one week in a cool place or the refrigerator and Caciocavello for up to two weeks.

Goat's Cheeses

Ranging in texture from soft and creamy to dry and sliceable, goat's milk cheeses are now made in countries all over the world. In France they are known as chèvre, the generic term for such cheeses. While they all share a dry, piquant aftertaste, their tangy – and unmistakably 'goaty' – flavour varies in strength according to the region of production, altitude, ripening period and mould cultures.

Traditionally produced on small farms or co-operatives throughout France and the Mediterranean, *chèvre* is made into a variety of small shapes: logs (*bûches*), dainty cylinders (*bûchettes*), little bells (*clochettes*) and an assortment of pyramids, discs and so on. The name *crottin* – which, you may or may not wish to know, means horse droppings! – refers to the shape of the small, hard, round goat's cheeses and also to their slightly darker colouring. Crottin de Chavignol is probably the best-known example and is highly prized for its bracingly sharp, full flavour.

In recent years goat's cheeses have become very popular in Britain, Australia and the United States, with many small cheesemakers producing their own unique versions. Montrachet is possibly the best-known American variety, while Kervella is produced in Western Australia and Chabis, Golden Cross, Roubiliac, Tymsboro' and many others in Britain.

CHOOSING AND STORING
Because there is such diversity and seasonal variance within this group, it is best to sample before you buy. That way, you will be sure that the degree of tartness, ripeness, dryness and so on is to your taste. Autumn and spring are particularly good times to buy, although crottin de Chavignol tends to be better in winter. Avoid tough-looking rinds unless, of course, you want a well-aged crottin. Don't buy cheeses with messy colouring or a rancid smell.

Many goat's cheeses are sold slightly underripe. Bear in mind that they will continue to mature and will ripen quickly if left beneath a cloche at a room temperature of, say, 20°C (68°F). If you want to hold the cheese at a particular stage of maturity, wrap it in foil and store it in an airtight container in the refrigerator. Most goat's cheeses will keep well in this way for at least a week.

Blue Cheeses

Blue cheeses acquire their characteristic veining from mould spores. These may be introduced to the milk before it is soured and then encouraged to develop during ripening, when the cheese is pierced with fine needles. This allows the air in so the mould can spread.

The most noble blue cheese must surely be Roquefort. Some 2,000 years ago it acquired its veining from the natural *Penicillium glaucum*, which thrived in the limestone caves of the Combalou plateau in France. In 1411 Charles VI bestowed a royal charter upon these caves, thereby initiating the Roquefort *appellation*, or quality control, which still exists today. Unusually for a blue cheese, Roquefort is made with sheep's milk, which is partly responsible for its pungent flavour. In cookery, its assertiveness works wonderfully well with other robust ingredients.

Italy's champion blue cheese is Gorgonzola, which is milder, softer and less salty than Roquefort. Both cheeses have very little rind.

Britain's most illustrious example is Stilton, of which the finest is Colston Bassett Stilton. It has a distinctive rind and is moist and creamy. More recent British blues include Dunsyre Blue (cow's milk) and Lanark Blue (sheep's milk) from Scotland, and Harbourne Blue (goat's milk) and Beenleigh Blue (sheep's milk) from Devon.

Ireland's most famous is Cashel Blue which, like Roquefort and Gorgonzola, has a foil-wrapped rind. Its particularly creamy texture blends smoothly in cooking. Other soft-textured blues that cook well include the American Oregon Blue and Maytag Blue.

CHOOSING AND STORING
Choose Roquefort in its prime, that is from around six months old. In perfect condition it will have a creamy, moist, virtually white paste and a uniform greenish-blue veining. It should have just a faint smell of mould. These guidelines apply to most blue cheeses that are wrapped in foil, except their paste is not quite as ivory-white as that of Roquefort and some of them reach maturity at only three months.

Gorgonzola should be springy to the touch and never brownish and hard. Contrary to popular belief, it should not have a pungent smell. Stilton should be creamy-ivory, with an even distribution of greenish-blue veining. It should be open-textured and never dry, hard or salty.

Wrap all foil-finished blue cheeses except Gorgonzola in a double layer of foil and keep them in an airtight container in the refrigerator. Gorgonzola is better wrapped in a damp cloth and stored in a cool place. All these cheeses should stay in good condition for 8 to 12 days. Be sure to bring them back to room temperature before serving.

The best way to store Stilton is wrapped in a linen cloth in a cool cellar or larder. Moisten the cloth if the cheese starts to dry out. If these conditions are impracticable, store it as for Roquefort.

The Cheeseboard

The cheeseboard in a good restaurant will offer 10 to 15 varieties of cheese, chosen for their different characters and strengths. At home, it is better to have a small selection of cheeses in their prime than a large number in poor condition. A small selection is also less confusing to the palate, enabling your guests to relish each cheese to the full. It generally makes sense to offer one hard or semi-hard cheese, one semi-soft and one blue.

If possible, buy from a good cheese shop, where the cheeses are properly stored and staff will be able to advise you. As a change, it can be fun to put together an alternative cheeseboard – see pages 183–9 for ideas.

Bring refrigerated cheeses to room temperature for at least an hour before serving to allow the full flavour to develop. However, the prepared cheeseboard should not be left in a warm room for more than 40 minutes, otherwise the cheeses may sweat. One way of overcoming this is to put the cheeses on the board and cover them with a damp cloth. I like only wooden boards, and I provide a separate knife for each cheese to prevent the different flavours intermingling.

There is an art to cutting cheese so that the cheeseboard continues to look appetizing and wastage is minimized. Small square or round cheeses, such as Camembert, should be cut in half (diagonally if it is a square cheese) and then into small triangular wedges. It used to be considered bad manners to cut the 'nose' off a wedge of Brie, and it certainly leaves an unappetizing piece of rind. Instead, long slices should be taken from alternate sides so that it maintains its shape. Tall, thin pieces of cheese, such as a wedge from a whole Cheddar, can be laid on their side, making it easier to cut off long slices. Finally, truckles such as Stilton need to have a 'lid' cut off the top. You can then either slice off whole rounds or score a line round the cheese a few centimetres from the top and cut down to give small wedges. Replace the lid when storing the cheese.

What to serve with cheese? I prefer something simple such as crusty bread and perhaps some tart grapes, crisp apples or ripe pears. I avoid biscuits and butter since I am not convinced that they enhance the cheese. Occasionally, though, I do like to serve a good chutney with a farmhouse Cheddar or similar cheese (see pages 186–8).

Here are my twelve favourite cheeseboards for the year. I have aimed for a good balance of texture, colour and taste in each one and have brought in seasonal cheeses at their peak.

January
Lancashire
Pouligny-Saint-Pierre
Fourme d'Ambert
Explorateur

February
Jersey Blue
Celtic Promise
Beaufort
Selles-sur-Cher

March
Gospel Green
Capricorn
Epoisses
Brillat-Savarin

April
Swaledale
Reblochon
Saint-Christophe
Shropshire Blue

May
Montgomery's Cheddar
Pierre-Robert
Tornegus
Crottin de Chavignol

June
Pavé d'Affinois
Smoked Gubbeen
Appleby's Cheshire
Roquefort

July
Isle of Avalon
Livarot
Saint-Marcellin
Pen-y-Bont

August
Cashel Blue
Banon
Milleens
Valençay

September
Maroilles
Appleby's Cheshire
Vacherin Mont d'Or
Lanark Blue

October
Wensleydale
Münster
Chaource
Roubiliac

November
Dunsyre Blue
Saint-Nectaire
Tomme de Savoie
Saint-Christophe

December
Stilton
Beaufort
Pérail
Vacherin

Serving Wine with Cheese

Alain Senderens, the well-known Parisian chef-restaurateur, regards the partnership of cheese and wine as so important that he displays a list of famous cheese and wine marriages in his restaurant. Ultimately, however, personal taste should play a part – although a few general rules hold good, such as strong cheeses need a full-bodied wine while mild ones are better matched with a light wine.

One common fallacy that I am happy to ignore is that all cheese goes with all red wine. This isn't the case. You must take into account the individual nature of both the cheese and the wine. Blanket statements about cheese and wine being good companions refer to everyday or indifferent wines. Certainly if a wine has negative qualities, these will be masked by cheese, especially a strong-flavoured one. By the same token, a powerful cheese will overwhelm the exquisite subtleties of a fine wine.

That said, there are many magical partnerships that are very easy to get right, particularly if you are looking for a match for a decent red wine – perhaps one that has been carried over from the main course. In this case, you could choose from the many hard and semi-hard cheeses, such as Gruyère, Beaufort, Comté, Emmenthal, Appenzel, mild Cheddar, Cheshire and fontina to name a few. You might also pick your way carefully around the semi-soft and soft cheeses. Among the soft fermented cheeses, Reblochon and Pont l'Évêque are probably the best bet, but only if they have been well cared for and remain delicate – almost sweet – in flavour. Be very cautious if you want to include Camembert and Brie; when ripe, these cheeses can acquire an acrid taste of ammonia that will kill good wine. It is best not to buy them too far in advance because they deteriorate rapidly after a day or two.

If you are serving a Sancerre or Pouilly Fumé with the main course and suspect it will be carried over to the cheese course, then you have the opportunity to enjoy one of the world's most sublime cheese and wine alliances, that of white goat's cheese and flinty white wine. With a selection of at least six goat's milk cheeses, you can create a cheeseboard that is visually very exciting, particularly if you line the board, or a large flat-bottomed basket, with glossy green vine leaves, or plane tree or chestnut leaves.

One of the great challenges of the cheeseboard is finding a match for strong, salty, blue cheese, whose aggressive nature has a distinctly discouraging effect on fine red wines. Roquefort, for example, despite its wondrous qualities, will completely annihilate most wines. However, most blue cheeses – and Roquefort in particular – make good partners for Sauternes and other dessert wines. So you can serve Sauternes with the dessert course, then continue the wine into the cheese course.

If you don't plan to offer a dessert wine, port goes well with strong blues, especially Stilton. If you're particularly keen on having a red wine, you could try a powerful, full-bodied one such as Zinfandel or, for special occasions, Gigondas or Côte Rotie.

A young-to-middle-aged Gorgonzola or Bresse Bleu, or a milder blue such as dolcelatte or dolcelatte torta, is a good match for a Zinfandel, Barolo or Barbaresco. A well-aged Gorgonzola, however, would probably be too challenging in its pungency and sharpness even for such robust wines.

Cooking with Cheese

All cheeses have unique characteristics but there are a few points to bear in mind when deciding which to cook with. Generally I find I use fresh cheeses more in summer for light dishes and desserts and in winter harder cheeses, which add warmth and depth of flavour. Hard cheeses such as Parmesan, Cheddar and Gruyère are the most popular for cooking. Their good melting qualities make them ideal for sauces, pasta and gratins. Blue cheeses lend real depth of flavour to dishes, and pungent ones such as Roquefort should be added sparingly. Soft rinded cheeses such as Brie and Camembert types are not often used in cooking because their large proportion of rind makes them wasteful. However, they are delicious melted on top of soups or bread and can also be grilled or baked whole. Goat's cheeses are increasingly popular and are very versatile – try them in salads, pizzas, sauces, stuffings and even desserts.

Cheese reacts differently depending on how it is cooked. The main principle is that it should not be exposed to too fierce a heat – except when grilling, in which case the cooking time should be brief. Overcooked cheese tends to be rubbery. Above a certain temperature the protein coagulates, separating the fat and water to produce a stringy texture. The secret is to add the cheese towards the end of cooking. If you are using it in a sauce, always take the pan off the heat and allow the cheese to melt in.

Hard cheeses can withstand higher temperatures than soft ones. Varieties such as haloumi, feta and mozzarella are best cooked quickly at a high temperature. The classic example is mozzarella cooked in the blazing heat of a traditional pizza oven. The high fat or water content of soft cheeses means they blend easily with liquid, making them useful for vinaigrettes and other uncooked sauces (see the recipe for Goat's Cheese and Cumin Vinaigrette on page 20).

Finally, a couple of tips: when grating cheese, chill it first to firm it up as this makes the job easier. And take care when seasoning cheese dishes as most cheeses contain added salt – taste first.

Cheese and Your Health

Cheese can make a valuable contribution to our diet, supplying generous amounts of protein, vitamin A and calcium, which helps prevent osteoporosis. It also contains vitamins B2, B12 and D, niacin and folic acid, as well as phosphorus and zinc. It is beneficial to children, because calcium aids the growth of strong bones and teeth, and also to the elderly, because it provides a concentration of nutrients that might otherwise be lacking in their diet. The vitamin B12 is especially welcome for vegetarians, who may like to seek out types made with a vegetarian rennet substitute rather than traditional rennet – a substance extracted from the stomach lining of calves to clot the milk.

There's no denying, however, that many cheeses are high in fat – a cause of dietary concern for most of us nowadays. But I do believe it's possible to enjoy cheese as part of a healthy diet. As in all things, moderation is the key. Set out to discover the wealth of artisan cheeses on offer and enjoy them just two or three times a week. This is more satisfying than consuming bland, plastic-wrapped, factory-produced cheeses on a daily basis. A lump of good farmhouse cheese, a hunk of bread and some salad make for a fulfilling meal and you won't need butter or any other form of fat with it.

In cooking, it really pays to use good-quality cheeses. If you add a farmhouse Cheddar to your cheese sauce rather than a factory one, for example, you will find the taste is so much stronger that you can get away with using less. The farmhouse version may be more expensive but you will save on both calories and cost.

Soft ripened cheeses such as Brie and Camembert are not as calorific as you might think, containing around two-thirds the fat of hard cheeses such as Cheddar and only half the fat of Stilton. And, of course, there are cheeses that are naturally low-fat, mainly the soft ones such as ricotta, fromage frais, cottage cheese and quark. You will find recipes for all of these in this book. But please, don't use the half-fat cheeses on sale in some supermarkets. These may have only half the fat but they have absolutely none of the flavour.

Several years ago, an irrational fear developed in Britain about the health risks of unpasteurized cheeses, which were wrongly seen as causing listeriosis. Since then, the government's Chief Medical Officer has completely exonerated unpasteurized cheeses, and, mercifully, they are just as safe to eat as pasteurized ones. However, there is a slight risk of listeriosis from rinded and mould-ripened cheeses (e.g. Camembert and Stilton), whether pasteurized or unpasteurized. Government advice is that these should be avoided by pregnant women, the very young, the very old, and anyone suffering from an immune-deficiency illness.

TYPICAL NUTRITION VALUES IN POPULAR CHEESES PER 100g

Cheese	Carbohydrates (g)	Fat (g)	Protein (g)	Calories (Kcal)
Brie	Trace	26.9	19.3	319
Camembert	Trace	23.7	20.9	297
Chaumes	1.0	25.4	21.0	317
Cheddar	0.1	34.4	25.5	410
Chèvre	Trace	25.6	21.0	314
Danish blue	1.0	29.0	20.0	336
Dolcelatte	Trace	36.0	17.3	394
Edam	Trace	24.1	27.1	326
Feta	3.0	24.2	17.2	298
Fontina	0.1	30.45	25.2	381
Gorgonzola	Trace	26.0	19.0	333
Gouda	Trace	31.0	24.0	375
Gruyère	0.8	32.0	28.0	403
Mascarpone	4.8	40.30	5.5	404
Mozzarella (full-fat)	Trace	25.4	18.0	301
Mozzarella (half-fat)	1.8	10.5	20.0	182
Parmesan	Trace	32.7	39.4	452
Pont L'Évêque	Trace	22.5	24.0	299
Ricotta (full-fat)	2.6	14.8	10.0	185
Roquefort	1.8	29.0	21.0	352
Stilton	0.1	35.5	22.7	411

Notes on the Recipes

● Butter is always unsalted.
● Eggs are large free-range.
● In white sauces, boiled milk is often specified. Although this is not essential, bringing the milk to the boil and then straining it before adding it to the sauce gives a smoother finish.
● Metric, imperial and American measurements are given in that order; use any one but do not combine them.

● Alternative cheeses are suggested in most recipes. These are recommended replacements if the cheese in the ingredients list is hard to find, or Australian or American equivalents for readers in those countries.

Occasionally, though, I have suggested a completely different cheese. This is to give a new twist to the existing recipe – for example, replacing the Cheddar in a soup with goat's cheese or Stilton. Feel free to experiment.

IMPORTANT

Some of the recipes contain raw or lightly cooked eggs, which may carry a slight risk of salmonella poisoning. These should be avoided by the very young, the very old, anyone suffering from an immune-deficiency illness, and pregnant women.

Because of the marginal risk of listeriosis, it is also advisable that these groups steer clear of rinded and mould-ripened cheeses.

BASICS

Vegetable Stock

MAKES about 1 litre
(1¾ pints, 4 cups)

2 tablespoons olive oil
1 onion, chopped
1 small leek, chopped
75g (3oz, ½ cup) celeriac, chopped
2 large carrots, chopped
1 celery stick, chopped
75g (3oz, ¾ cup) white cabbage, chopped
½ head fennel, chopped
4 garlic cloves, chopped
125ml (4 fl oz, ½ cup) white wine (optional)
4 black peppercorns
1 sprig of fresh thyme
1 bay leaf
1.5 litres (2½ pints, 6¼ cups) water
2 teaspoons salt

There are as many different recipes for vegetable stock as there are cooks, but most of them contain sweet-tasting vegetables such as carrots and leeks.

Heat the oil in a large saucepan, add all the vegetables and the garlic and cook gently for about 5 minutes, until softened. Add the wine, if using, then add the peppercorns, thyme, bay leaf and water.

Bring to the boil, add the salt and simmer for 40 minutes, until reduced by a third of its original volume. Strain through a fine sieve and leave to cool. Refrigerate until required or freeze.

P.G. TIPS You can now buy cartons of chilled fresh stock in supermarkets. These are generally of good quality and can be used in all the recipes requiring stock in this book. However, some of them are quite salty, so be careful when adding seasoning. Home-made stocks are, of course, considerably cheaper.

Chicken Stock

MAKES about 1.75 litres
(3 pints, 7½ cups)

2.3kg (5lb) raw chicken carcasses, or chicken wings & legs
350g (12oz, 2½ cups) onions, chopped
350g (12oz, 1½ cups) carrots, chopped
150g (5oz, generous 1 cup) celery, chopped
1 leek, chopped
1 bouquet garni (see Tip)

A light, clear, refined chicken stock, ideal for sauces and soups.

Put the chicken carcasses in a large saucepan, cover with cold water and bring slowly to the boil. Skim off any impurities that rise to the surface, then add the vegetables and bouquet garni. Simmer very gently for 4 hours, then strain through a fine sieve and leave to cool. Refrigerate the stock until it is required or freeze.

P.G. TIPS To make a bouquet garni, tie together 1 bay leaf and 2 sprigs each of fresh parsley and thyme and wrap in a small strip of green of leek.

Cheese-infused Chicken Stock

MAKES about 1 litre
(1¾ pints, 4 cups)

15g (½ oz, 1 tablespoon) unsalted butter

1 onion, sliced

1 leek, sliced

2 garlic cloves, peeled & halved

1 litre (1¾ pints, 4 cups) Chicken Stock (see opposite)

A few sprigs each of fresh parsley, rosemary & thyme

100g (4oz, ½ cup) rinds of hard cheese

This is ideal for using up those last pieces of cheese and rind that are left after grating as much as you can from a piece. Parmesan is perfect for this recipe. The cheese adds a wonderfully rich flavour to the stock, which can be used as a base for risottos, pastas, sauces and soups.

Heat the butter in a heavy-based pan, add the onion, leek and garlic and cook over a gentle heat until softened. Add the chicken stock, herbs and cheese rind and bring to the boil.

Reduce the heat and simmer for 20 minutes, then strain through a fine sieve and leave to cool. Refrigerate the stock until it is required or freeze.

Meat Stock

MAKES about 1.75 litres
(3 pints, 7½ cups)

90ml (3 fl oz, ⅓ cup) vegetable oil

900g (2lb) beef or veal bones, chopped into small pieces

450g (1lb) beef or veal trimmings, cut into small pieces

3 carrots, chopped

2 onions, chopped

1 celery stick, chopped

2 garlic cloves, crushed

50g (2oz, ¼ cup) tomato purée

1 bouquet garni (see Tip opposite)

You can use beef or veal bones to make this, but veal give a better flavour.

Preheat the oven to 220°C, 425°F, gas 7. Heat half the oil in a roasting tin, add the bones and roast them for about 30 minutes, until well browned. Meanwhile, heat the remaining oil in a large, deep pan and fry the meat trimmings until very well browned.

Add the bones, vegetables and garlic to the pan, cover with water and bring slowly to the boil. Skim off any impurities that rise to the surface. Stir in the tomato purée and bouquet garni and simmer over a very low heat for 2 hours, skimming frequently. Strain through a fine sieve and leave to cool. Refrigerate until required or freeze.

Reduced Meat Stock

Pour the strained meat stock into a pan and boil until reduced by half its volume. Store or freeze as above.

Basic Cheese Sauce (Sauce Mornay)

MAKES about 600ml
(1 pint, 2½ cups)

900ml (1½ pints, 3¾ cups) milk
1 onion, peeled & studded with 3-4 cloves
50g (2oz, 4 tablespoons) unsalted butter
50g (2oz, ½ cup) plain flour
100g (4oz, 1 cup) Gruyère, grated
1 teaspoon Dijon mustard
Freshly grated nutmeg
125ml (4 fl oz, ½ cup) double cream
2 egg yolks
Salt & freshly ground black pepper

ALTERNATIVE CHEESES

For an interestingly different sauce, replace the Gruyère with a goat's cheese or blue cheese

This is a classic white sauce that has been enriched with cream and egg and includes Gruyère cheese.

Put the milk and onion in a pan and bring to the boil, then remove from the heat and leave to stand for 5 minutes. Melt the butter in a separate pan and stir in the flour to make a *roux*. Cook gently, stirring, for 2-3 minutes.

Remove the onion from the milk and add the milk to the *roux* a little at a time, stirring constantly. Bring slowly to the boil, then reduce the heat and cook very gently for 20 minutes, stirring from time to time to prevent sticking.

Remove from the heat, add the cheese and stir until melted. Add the mustard and season with nutmeg, salt and pepper. If you like, strain through a fine sieve for a smoother sauce. Stir in the cream and egg yolks.

Rapid Cheese Sauce

SERVES 4

125ml (4 fl oz, ½ cup) Vegetable Stock (see page 16)
125ml (4 fl oz, ½ cup) double cream
40g (1½ oz, scant ½ cup) Parmesan, freshly grated
2 teaspoons arrowroot
75g (3oz, 6 tablespoons) chilled unsalted butter, cut into small pieces
Salt & freshly ground black pepper

This sauce is simple to make and the result is both satisfying and tasty.

Bring the vegetable stock and cream to the boil and boil for 2-3 minutes. Put the cheese and arrowroot in a bowl and mix to a paste with a little water. Add to the stock and stir over a gentle heat until thickened. Whisk in the butter a few pieces at a time until smooth and creamy. Season to taste and serve straight away.

P.G.TIPS To serve this sauce with fish, you can make it taste more interesting by adding fresh herbs such as chervil, chives and tarragon.

Cheese Butters

SERVE 4

These can be prepared well ahead of time and stored in the refrigerator or even the freezer. You can then cut off slices to use as required – perhaps as a topping for grilled fish, steak or vegetables.

Camembert Butter

MAKES 190g
(6½oz, about ¾ cup)

¼ Camembert, rind removed
125g (4½ oz, generous ½ cup) softened
unsalted butter
Freshly ground black pepper

Process all the ingredients together in a blender or food processor, then scrape out on to a piece of foil. Shape into a log and roll up in the foil, then chill until required.

Roquefort Butter

MAKES 250g
(9oz, generous 1 cup)

100g (4oz, ½ cup) Roquefort
150g (5oz, 10 tablespoons) softened
unsalted butter
1 tablespoon chopped fresh parsley
Freshly ground black pepper

Prepare as for Camembert Butter.

Roquefort &
Green Peppercorn Butter

Stir 1 tablespoon crushed green peppercorns into the Roquefort Butter.

Ricotta, Lemon Thyme &
Garlic Butter

MAKES 225g (8oz, 1 cup)

100g (4oz, ½ cup) ricotta
100g (4oz, ½ cup) softened
unsalted butter
1 garlic clove, crushed
1 tablespoon fresh lemon thyme leaves

Prepare as for Camembert Butter.

Coriander & Goat's Cheese Pesto

MAKES about 300ml
(½ pint, 1¼ cups)

1 garlic clove, crushed

50g (2oz, 1 cup) fresh coriander leaves

1 tablespoon pine kernels

150ml (¼ pint, ⅔ cup) extra-virgin olive oil

2 tablespoons freshly grated Parmesan

75g (3oz, scant ½ cup) soft mild goat's cheese, such as Sainte-Maure, Golden Cross or Roubiliac

50g (2oz, ¼ cup) mascarpone

Salt & freshly ground black pepper

ALTERNATIVE
CHEESES

Kervella (Aust), Montrachet (US) or any other soft goat's cheese

Throughout this book you will discover the versatility of this sauce. It is wonderful with fresh pasta and can also be used as a stuffing for vegetables, fish or chicken if you halve the amount of olive oil. You could also vary the herbs, replacing the coriander with basil, for example, or with a combination of fresh herbs.

Put the garlic, coriander and pine kernels in a blender and blitz to a purée, gradually adding the olive oil. Add the cheeses and blend again until the mixture has a thick, saucelike consistency. Season with salt and pepper.

Goat's Cheese & Cumin Vinaigrette

MAKES about 300ml
(½ pint, 1¼ cups)

100g (4oz, ½ cup) soft mild goat's cheese such as Golden Cross

2 tablespoons hot water

2 tablespoons red wine vinegar

½ tablespoon ground cumin

1 tablespoon chopped fresh oregano (optional)

1 egg yolk

100ml (3½ fl oz, scant ½ cup) vegetable oil or groundnut oil

Salt & freshly ground black pepper

This unusual vinaigrette can be served with spring vegetable salads and is also delicious with Carpaccio of Beef (see page 48) as an alternative to the dolcelatte mustard dressing.

Put the goat's cheese in a bowl, pour on the hot water and beat until smooth and creamy. Add the vinegar, cumin, oregano, if using, and egg yolk and whisk together until blended. Gradually whisk in the oil and then season to taste, being careful with the amount of salt you add as some goat's cheeses have a rather salty flavour.

Quark Mayonnaise

SERVES 4

2 egg yolks
2 tablespoons red wine vinegar
4 (5) tablespoons olive oil
225g (8oz, 1 cup) quark
2 tablespoons water
Salt & freshly ground black pepper

ALTERNATIVE

CHEESES

Low-fat fromage frais or ricotta

Quark is extremely low in fat and so is very useful for anyone trying to reduce their fat intake – for whom mayonnaise would usually be out of bounds because of all the oil it contains. Although this recipe includes a little olive oil for flavour, most of it is replaced by quark, resulting in an altogether healthier mayonnaise with a smooth consistency and delicate taste.

Whisk the egg yolks and vinegar with a pinch of salt until creamy. Whisk in the oil a little at a time, as if making mayonnaise, to form a light emulsion. Blend the quark with the water and add to the egg mixture, then season to taste with salt and pepper.

Shortcrust Pastry

MAKES 450g (1lb)

250g (9oz, generous 2 cups) plain flour
175g (6oz, ¾ cup) chilled unsalted butter, cut into small pieces
1 egg, beaten
A pinch of salt

To make cheese pastry, add 3 (4) tablespoons freshly grated Parmesan to the flour with the butter.

Sift the flour on to a work surface or into a large bowl. Add the butter and blend together with your fingertips until it has a soft, sandy texture. Make a well in the centre and add the beaten egg and salt. Gently mix together with your fingertips to form a smooth, even dough. Wrap in cling film and chill for about 30 minutes or until required.

Sweet Pastry

MAKES 675g (1½lb)

350g (12oz, 3 cups) plain flour
225g (8oz, 1 cup) unsalted butter, cut into small pieces (at room temperature)
A pinch of salt
100g (4oz, 1 cup) icing sugar, sifted
Finely grated zest of ½ lemon
1 egg, beaten

This rich pastry is suitable for most sweet tarts.

Sift the flour on to a work surface and make a well in the centre. Put the butter, salt, sugar and lemon zest in the well and then add the egg. With your fingertips, gradually bring the flour into the centre until all the ingredients come together to form a soft dough. Knead very lightly for 1 minute, until completely smooth, then form the dough into a ball. Wrap in cling film and chill for 2 hours.

Brioche

10g (⅓ oz) fresh yeast
2 tablespoons milk
450g (1lb, 4 cups) strong plain flour
1 teaspoon salt
20g (¾ oz, 1½ tablespoons) caster sugar
4 eggs
100g (4oz, ½ cup) softened unsalted butter
1 egg beaten with 1 tablespoon of milk, to glaze

This quick and easy brioche is great for breakfast but can also be used in both savoury and sweet dishes, such as Warm Brioche of Goat's Cheese with Minted Leeks (see page 40) and Croque Mademoiselle (see page 178).

Dissolve the yeast in the milk. Sift the flour, salt and sugar on to a work surface and make a well in the centre. Beat the eggs with the yeast mixture, then pour them into the well in the flour. Gradually work the flour into the eggs with the heel of your hand until a soft dough is formed, then knead it for 2–3 minutes. Work in the softened butter, using the same method, and knead for about 10 minutes or until the dough has a smooth texture. It will feel slightly sticky to the touch. Cover with cling film and leave to rest in the refrigerator for 30 minutes.

Shape the dough into 12 balls and place in buttered individual brioche tins. Or shape it into a loaf and place in a medium loaf tin. Cover and leave in a warm place for 30–40 minutes, until doubled in size. Preheat the oven to 200°C, 400°F, gas 6.

Brush the brioche with the beaten egg and milk mixture and bake until golden brown – about 20 minutes for brioche buns, 40 minutes for a loaf. Turn out on to a wire rack to cool.

Cheddar & Onion Loaf

1 heaped teaspoon fresh yeast
125ml (4 fl oz, ½ cup) water
2 teaspoons vegetable oil
275g (10oz, 2½ cups) strong plain flour
A pinch of salt
A pinch of sugar
1 egg, beaten
50g (2oz, scant ½ cup) onion, finely diced
175g (6oz, 1½ cups) mature farmhouse Cheddar, grated
25g (1oz, ¼ cup) Parmesan, freshly grated

This loaf (see photograph on page 189) is very quick to make as it needs only one rising. Although most recipes tell you to use warm water when making bread, I find cold water works perfectly well. In fact it is probably safer, since if the water is too hot it may kill the yeast and prevent the loaf rising.

Put the yeast in a small bowl, add the water and stir until the yeast has dissolved. Stir in the oil. Sift the flour, salt and sugar into a bowl and make a well in the centre. Pour in the yeast liquid and half the beaten egg and then stir in the flour to make a soft dough. Turn out on to a lightly floured work surface and knead for 8–10 minutes, until smooth and elastic. Leave to relax for 2–3 minutes, then work in the diced onion and grated cheeses and knead for about 2 minutes, until they are fully incorporated. Shape the dough into a loaf and place it in a greased 450g (1lb) loaf tin. Cover with a damp tea towel and leave in a warm place for about 1 hour, until doubled in size.

Preheat the oven to 220°C, 425°F, gas 7. Brush the top of the loaf with the remaining beaten egg and bake for 25–30 minutes, until the bread is golden brown and sounds hollow when turned out of the tin and tapped underneath. Turn out on to a wire rack to cool.

Stilton Bread

MAKES 2 LOAVES
....

20g (¾ oz) fresh yeast
300ml (½ pint, 1¼ cups) water
2 teaspoons malt extract
2 teaspoons golden syrup
500g (1lb 2oz, 4½ cups) strong plain flour
2 teaspoons salt
150g (5oz, generous ½ cup) Colston
Bassett Stilton, crumbled

This is an excellent way of using up those tiny bits of crumbled Stilton or other blue cheeses. Colston Bassett Stilton is a true jewel in Britain's cheesemaking revival. It may seem extravagant to use it in bread, but as the flavour is strong you don't need very much. (See the photograph on page 189.)

Put the yeast in a small bowl, add a little of the water and stir to dissolve. Stir in the malt extract and golden syrup. Sift the flour and salt into a bowl and make a well in the centre. Pour in the yeast liquid and the remaining water and then stir in the flour to make a soft dough. Turn out on to a lightly floured work surface and knead for 8–10 minutes, until smooth and elastic. Return to the cleaned bowl, cover with a damp tea towel and leave in a warm place for about 50 minutes, until doubled in size.

Punch down the dough and divide it in half. Roll out each piece into a rectangle about 20 x 30cm (8 x 12in). Sprinkle the Stilton evenly over the dough and roll up tightly. Place in 2 greased 450g (1lb) loaf tins or shape into rounds and place on greased baking sheets. Cover with a damp tea towel and leave in a warm place, until risen. Preheat the oven to 200°C, 400°F, gas 6.

Sprinkle the loaves with a little flour and bake for 35–40 minutes, until the bread is golden brown on top and sounds hollow when turned out of the tin and tapped underneath. Turn out on to a wire rack to cool.

Italian Picnic Loaf

MAKES 1 LOAF
....

1 tablespoon olive oil
2 garlic cloves, crushed
50g (2oz, 1 cup) sun-dried tomatoes in oil,
drained & finely chopped
2 tablespoons chopped black olives
1 quantity of Brioche dough
(see opposite)
1 ball of cow's milk mozzarella, well
drained & cut into slices 5mm (¼ in) thick
Butter, for greasing
1 tablespoon freshly grated Parmesan
A little milk, for brushing

Brioche dough is spread with mozzarella, olives and sun-dried tomatoes and then rolled up, producing an attractive and colourful spiral pattern when the loaf is sliced. It's a wonderful bread to take on picnics, fresh from the oven.

Heat half the olive oil in a small pan, add the garlic and cook gently for about 1 minute, until softened but not browned. Stir in the sun-dried tomatoes and olives and cook for 1 minute longer, then leave to cool.

Roll out the brioche dough into a 25cm (10in) square. Brush with the remaining olive oil, then arrange the mozzarella in overlapping slices over the top, starting 5cm (2in) in from the edge of the dough. Sprinkle over the olive and tomato mixture, then roll up the brioche tightly like a Swiss roll.

Lightly butter a large loaf tin and dust it with the grated Parmesan. Put the brioche roll in the tin, cover with a damp tea towel and leave in a warm place for 25 minutes, until risen and puffy. Preheat the oven to 200°C, 400°F, gas 6.

Brush the loaf with a little milk and then bake for 25 minutes, until it is golden brown on top and sounds hollow when turned out of the tin and tapped underneath. Serve warm.

Chapter One

Taramasalata with Cream Cheese on Tapenade Crostini

SERVES 4

3 slices of white bread, crusts removed

1 garlic clove, crushed

100g (4oz) smoked cod's roe, skinned

75g (3oz, scant ½ cup) cream cheese

3 (4) tablespoons lemon juice

6 (8) tablespoons olive oil

2 tablespoons tapenade

8 slices of crusty French bread, about 1cm (½ in) thick

Salt & freshly ground black pepper

My inclusion of cream cheese in this traditional Greek smoked fish purée would doubtless bring tears to the eyes of locals. I find it mellows and rounds the smoky flavour of the roe – try it and see what you think.

Soak the white bread in a little water or, better still, milk for 5 minutes. Squeeze out the excess moisture, then place the bread in a blender or food processor. Add the garlic, cod's roe and cream cheese and blitz to a smooth purée. Add the lemon juice and 4 (5) tablespoons of the olive oil and blend again, then transfer to a bowl. Season to taste, then chill for at least 2 hours.

To serve, mix the tapenade with the remaining olive oil. Toast the French bread, spread it with the taramasalata and drizzle over the tapenade.

P.G.TIPS

Jars of tapenade, a black olive and anchovy paste, are readily available in supermarkets and delicatessens and the quality is usually quite good. Green olive tapenade works just as well. I like to serve these crostini with pre-dinner drinks or with a tipple of Ouzo. And why not?

Twice-roasted Red Peppers with Haloumi, Capers & Olives

SERVES 4

4 large red peppers
4 (5) tablespoons olive oil
2 garlic cloves, thinly sliced
2 tablespoons chopped fresh flat-leaf parsley
12 black olives, stoned & halved
2 tablespoons superfine capers, rinsed & drained
8 slices of haloumi, 1cm (½ in) thick
Salt & freshly ground black pepper

For the dressing
2 tablespoons white wine vinegar
125ml (4 fl oz, ½ cup) olive oil
¼ teaspoon Dijon mustard
½ small red chilli, deseeded & finely chopped

ALTERNATIVE
CHEESE

Feta

The vibrant colours of this dish are almost as enticing as its robust flavours. Although I usually serve it warm, it is also very good cold. Substitute oregano or basil for the parsley, if you like.

Preheat the oven to 200°C, 400°F, gas 6. Cut the peppers in half lengthways, brush with a little of the olive oil and season with salt and pepper. Bake for 1 hour or until tender. Remove from the oven and leave until cool enough to handle, then peel off the skin and cut the peppers lengthways into strips 2cm (¾ in) wide.

Lightly brush a gratin dish with olive oil. Put the pepper strips in it, sprinkle over the garlic, parsley, olives and capers and season with salt and pepper. Lay the haloumi cheese slices on top, drizzle over the remaining olive oil and return to the oven for 10–12 minutes, until the cheese is just starting to melt.

Meanwhile, whisk together all the ingredients for the dressing and season to taste. Remove the peppers from the oven and drizzle over the dressing. Serve warm, with herb-grilled crusty bread (see Tip below).

P.G.TIPS

To make herb-grilled crusty bread, brush slices of baguette with olive oil and sprinkle with chopped fresh herbs, then put under a hot grill until golden.

Feta & Roasted Pepper Mousse with Rocket & Pine Kernels

SERVES 4

1 large red pepper
150ml (¼ pint, ⅔ cup) olive oil
225g (8oz, 1 cup) Greek feta
200g (7oz scant 1 cup) Greek yoghurt
1 garlic clove, crushed
3 gelatine leaves
1 tablespoon balsamic vinegar
A handful of young rocket leaves
1 tablespoon pine kernels
Salt & freshly ground black pepper

This is my version of the Greek dish ktipiti, *which is usually a dip rather than a mousse. The saltiness of the feta cheese contrasts well with the peppery rocket.*

Preheat the oven to 200°C, 400°F, gas 6. Rub the pepper with 2 tablespoons of the olive oil, place on a baking tray and bake for 40 minutes or until tender. Leave until cool enough to handle, then peel off the skin, cut the pepper in half and remove the seeds. Put the pepper in a blender with the feta, yoghurt, garlic and 4 tablespoons of the olive oil and blitz to a fine purée.

Put the gelatine in a small pan, cover with about 3 tablespoons of water and leave for 5 minutes to soften. Melt over a gentle heat until clear. Stir it thoroughly into the purée and strain the mixture through a fine sieve. Season to taste and pour into 4 ramekin dishes or coffee cups. Chill for 1–2 hours, until set.

Whisk together the balsamic vinegar and the remaining olive oil to make a dressing and season to taste with salt and pepper. Unmould the mousses on to individual serving plates. Toss the rocket leaves and pine kernels with the dressing and arrange them around the mousses.

Emmenthal Corniottes with Marc de Bourgogne

MAKES ABOUT 20

250g (9oz, generous 1 cup) fromage blanc or cream cheese
150ml (¼ pint, ⅔ cup) crème fraîche
2 tablespoons Marc de Bourgogne
200g (7oz, 1¾ cups) Emmenthal, grated
2 eggs, beaten
Freshly grated nutmeg
1 quantity of shortcrust pastry (see page 21)
1 egg beaten with 2 tablespoons milk, to glaze
Salt & freshly ground black pepper

ALTERNATIVE

CHEESES

Swiss Appenzell or Gruyère

Corniottes are little triangular pastries which can be filled with sweet or savoury ingredients. Baked until crisp, they are a speciality of Burgundy, where they are served as a snack. If you don't have any Marc de Bourgogne, you could use kirsch instead.

Preheat the oven to 200°C, 400°F, gas 6. Put the fromage blanc or cream cheese, crème fraîche and Marc de Bourgogne in a bowl and beat in the grated Emmenthal and eggs to form a paste. Season with nutmeg, salt and pepper and set aside.

Roll out the pastry until it is 3mm (⅛ in) thick and cut out 10cm (4in) rounds – you should have about 20. Put some filling in the centre of each one, brush the edges with a little cold water and then pull 3 sides of the pastry up over the filling to form a point. Pinch together firmly to seal. Chill for up to 1 hour, then brush with the beaten egg and milk mixture and bake for 20–25 minutes, until golden. Serve hot or warm.

P.G. TIPS Smaller *corniottes* make great cocktail canapés. They also freeze successfully, so they can be prepared in advance and baked straight from the freezer when required. Puff pastry works just as well as shortcrust pastry.

Pressed Leek Terrine with Cashel Blue & Green Peppercorns

SERVES 8-10

30 young leeks

A pinch of sugar

250g (9oz, generous 1 cup) Cashel Blue, crumbled

2 tablespoons green peppercorns

2 hard-boiled eggs, whites & yolks separated & chopped

2 shallots, finely chopped

1 tablespoon chopped fresh tarragon

Salt & freshly ground black pepper

For the dressing

2 tablespoons champagne vinegar

8 (10) tablespoons walnut oil

½ teaspoon Dijon mustard

ALTERNATIVE
CHEESES

Any type of blue cheese is suitable. Try Bleu des Causses, Roquefort or Saint-Agur

I suggest you make this terrine for a special occasion as it takes a little while to prepare and should not be kept for long, otherwise its freshness and crispness will be lost.

Trim the leeks, wash them well and cut them into 20–25cm (8–10in) lengths. Bring a large pan of water to the boil with the sugar and some salt. Throw in the leeks, return to the boil and cook for 8–10 minutes, until just tender. Remove the leeks and cool slightly. Squeeze out all excess moisture and dry them in a cloth.

Take a loaf tin measuring about 20×7.5×7.5cm (8×3×3in) and line it with cling film, leaving a 5cm (2in) overhang on all sides. Cover the base with a layer of about 6–8 leeks (or more if needed), with the white parts at one end, and season with salt and pepper. Sprinkle over some of the cheese, peppercorns, white and yolk of egg, shallots and tarragon. Lay more leeks on top; the green tops should rest on the white part of the previous layer. Scatter with the filling ingredients as before and continue layering in this way, seasoning throughout, until the loaf tin is full. Finish with a layer of leeks. Fold over the overlapping cling film to cover the leeks.

Place a board that will just fit inside the tin on top of the leeks, and put a heavy weight (or a couple of cans) on top of that to compress the filling. Refrigerate overnight.

To serve, turn out the terrine and peel off the cling film. Using a sharp, long-bladed knife (or better still, an electric knife), cut the terrine into slices about 1cm (½in) thick and place on individual serving plates. Whisk together the ingredients for the dressing, season with salt and pepper and drizzle it around the slices of terrine.

Glazed Oysters on Crushed Potatoes with Parsley & Bleu d'Auvergne

SERVES 4

250g (9oz) new potatoes
4 (5) tablespoons milk
4 (5) tablespoons olive oil
2 tablespoons chopped fresh flat-leaf parsley
24 plump oysters
Salt & freshly ground black pepper

For the sauce
2 egg yolks
4 (5) tablespoons dry white wine
150ml (¼ pint, ⅔ cup) double cream
75g (3oz, scant ½ cup) Bleu d'Auvergne, crumbled

ALTERNATIVE
CHEESES

Roquefort, Maytag Blue (US) or Oregon Blue (US)

The combination of oysters and blue cheese may sound unexpected but it is a marriage made in culinary heaven. This is my version of a dish I came across at the Bel-Air Hotel in Los Angeles, during a week I spent there as guest chef. The original recipe used Maytag Blue, a creamy, salty cheese from Iowa, but I have substituted Bleu d'Auvergne.

Cook the potatoes in boiling salted water until just tender, then drain well. Place in a bowl, add the milk, olive oil and parsley and crush them coarsely with a fork. Season with salt and pepper and keep warm.

Open the oysters and remove from the shells, reserving the juices (see Tip below). Discard the top part of each shell and clean the bottom part.

For the sauce, whisk the egg yolks and wine together in a small bowl, then set the bowl over a pan of simmering water and whisk until the mixture thickens and doubles in volume. Boil the cream and cheese together for 2–3 minutes, then fold into the whisked egg yolk and wine mixture along with the strained oyster juices.

To serve, divide the crushed potatoes between the cleaned oyster shells. Season the oysters, put them on top of the potato mixture and then coat with the sauce. Place under a hot grill for 5 minutes, until golden (or place in a hot oven). Serve immediately.

P.G.TIPS
To open oysters you need an oyster knife or a short, strong-bladed knife. Wrap your hand in a tea towel to protect it, then take hold of an oyster and insert the knife blade between the shells, next to the hinge. Twist the knife to lever open the top shell, then cut the muscle connecting the oyster to the shell. Next, loosen the muscle connecting the oyster to the bottom shell. Take out the oyster and strain the juices into a bowl.

Parmesan Brioche Toast with Taleggio, Sautéed Plum Tomatoes & Oregano

SERVES 4

2 tablespoons olive oil

2 garlic cloves, crushed

450g (1lb) small plum tomatoes, halved

2 tablespoons chopped fresh oregano

2 eggs, beaten

100ml (3½ fl oz, ½ cup) milk

50g (2oz, ½ cup) Parmesan, freshly grated

Freshly grated nutmeg

4 slices of brioche (see page 22), cut 2cm (¾ in) thick

40g (1½ oz, 3 tablespoons) unsalted butter

4 (5) tablespoons aged Taleggio slivers

Salt & freshly ground black pepper

ALTERNATIVE CHEESES

Substitute freshly shaved Parmesan or Asiago for the Taleggio

This simple recipe is a savoury version of French toast. A good aged Taleggio cheese adds a creamy, aromatic and slightly sour flavour, which partners the sweetness of the tomatoes and brioche well. If yellow plum tomatoes are available, why not use half red, half yellow? The colours look stunning.

Heat the oil in a pan, add the garlic and cook for 1 minute. Add the tomatoes and sauté them until they begin to soften. Season with salt and pepper and stir in the oregano. Keep warm.

In a shallow bowl, whisk together the eggs, milk and Parmesan cheese, seasoning with a little nutmeg, salt and pepper. Cut the brioche slices into rounds, if liked, or leave them whole. Dip them in the egg mixture on both sides. Heat the butter in a frying pan, add the brioche and cook for 2–3 minutes on each side, until golden.

Put the Parmesan French toasts on serving plates and arrange the tomatoes on top. Scatter over the Taleggio and place under a hot grill to melt the cheese slightly before serving.

P.G.TIPS

It's important to use good, sweet, ripe tomatoes here. Plum tomatoes are generally fuller flavoured, but if they are not readily available, try using the larger, rounded varieties, sliced. Add a pinch of sugar if their flavour is not all it should be. White rolls or muffins can be substituted for the brioche.

PARMESAN BRIOCHE TOAST WITH TALEGGIO, SAUTÉED PLUM TOMATOES & OREGANO

Ratatouille-stuffed Mozzarella Wrapped in Prosciutto

SERVES 4

....

3 (4) tablespoons extra-virgin olive oil
1 small aubergine, sliced
1 courgette, sliced
1 garlic clove, crushed
1 teaspoon chopped fresh thyme
2 balls of cow's milk mozzarella
2 plum tomatoes, skinned & sliced
8 thin slices of prosciutto
50g (2oz, 4 tablespoons) unsalted butter
Salt & freshly ground black pepper

For the dressing
2 tablespoons balsamic vinegar
6 (8) tablespoons extra-virgin olive oil
1 tomato, skinned, deseeded & diced
½ tablespoon chopped black olives
6 fresh basil leaves, shredded

ALTERNATIVE
....
CHEESE
....
Provolone

Although buffalo mozzarella is generally held to be superior to cow's milk mozzarella, in this recipe I actually prefer to use the cow's milk cheese because it is less milky in texture and holds its shape better.

To make the ratatouille, heat the oil in a frying pan and fry the aubergine and courgette slices until tender. Stir in the garlic and thyme and cook for 1 minute, then season and leave to cool.

Cut each mozzarella horizontally into 4 equal slices and season lightly. Cover 4 slices with layers of aubergine, courgette and tomato, then top with the remaining cheese slices, making 4 ratatouille-stuffed mozzarella sandwiches in all. Wrap each one in 2 slices of prosciutto to secure the filling and chill for at least 30 minutes.

Heat the butter in a large frying pan, add the cheese sandwiches and fry until golden, about 2–3 minutes on each side. Place on 4 serving plates. Mix together all the ingredients for the dressing and season to taste. Pour it over the cheese sandwiches and serve straight away.

P.G.TIPS

Try grilling the stuffed mozzarella on a barbecue for a superb smoky flavour. Some people may be surprised to see that I do not advise salting the aubergine in this recipe. When slicing aubergines thinly, I really see little point in the exercise. However, when I use them in halves, I do usually salt them before cooking.

Roasted Aubergine Moutabel with Roubiliac & Thyme

SERVES 4

3 medium aubergines

2 tablespoons tahini (sesame seed paste)

1 garlic clove, crushed

1 teaspoon ground cumin

2 tablespoons lemon juice

1 Roubiliac goat's cheese log, cut into 12 slices

2 tablespoons fresh thyme leaves

4 (5) tablespoons walnut oil

Salt & freshly ground black pepper

ALTERNATIVE

CHEESE

Any soft fresh goat's cheese log

Moutabel is a Middle Eastern dish of puréed aubergine and tahini, also known as baba ghanoush. *I find aubergines have a great affinity with cheese. In this dish, aubergine halves are stuffed with a moutabel-style filling and then topped with goat's cheese and thyme. It is one of my favourite combinations. Serve on some salad leaves with a dressing of Middle Eastern flavours, such as a vinaigrette containing peeled, deseeded and finely diced tomato, chopped coriander and a little ground cumin.*

Preheat the oven to 190°C, 375°F, gas 5. Cut the aubergines in half, score the cut sides with a knife in a criss-cross pattern and bake for 45 minutes–1 hour, until tender. The exterior should be slightly charred but not burnt. Remove from the oven and leave to cool, then scoop out the flesh without damaging the skins. Chop the flesh very finely and mix it with the tahini, garlic, cumin, lemon juice and some salt and pepper.

Refill the aubergine skins with this mixture (there may only be enough to fill 4 halves), retaining the original shape of the aubergines. Put them in a lightly oiled, shallow ovenproof dish. Top each one with the slices of goat's cheese, sprinkle over the thyme leaves and drizzle with the walnut oil. Return to the oven for 8–10 minutes, until the cheese is golden and just beginning to melt. Cool slightly before serving.

Saganaki (Fried Sheep's Cheese with Lemon)

SERVES 4

75g (3oz, 6 tablespoons) unsalted butter

8 slices of kasseri or kefalotiri, cut 2cm (¾ in) thick

Juice of 1 lemon

Salt & freshly ground black pepper

ALTERNATIVE

CHEESE

Haloumi

This dish of simply fried sheep's milk cheese is served as a staple in tavernas throughout the Greek islands. Its beauty lies in its simplicity. It must be one of the easiest dishes to prepare, with just three ingredients, but it is delicious – and exceedingly moreish.

Heat the butter in a large frying pan until foaming, add the cheese slices and fry for 1–2 minutes on each side, until golden. Season lightly with salt and pepper and then pour the lemon juice over the cheese in the pan. Serve straight away, with lots of crusty bread.

P.G. TIPS **The lemon juice nicely flavours the butter, but to add an extra dimension I occasionally like to add fresh capers and herbs. In Greece the cheese is sometimes flamed with brandy at the table.**

Goyère

SERVES 4-6

450g (1lb, 2⅔ cups) potatoes, cut into
small cubes

25g (1oz, 2 tablespoons) unsalted butter

1 small onion, finely chopped

100g (4oz, ⅔ cup) smoked bacon, chopped

125g (4½ oz, generous ½ cup) Maroilles,
rind removed, cut into 5mm (¼ in) dice

2 eggs, beaten

100ml (3½ fl oz, ½ cup) crème fraîche
or double cream

Salt & freshly ground black pepper

For the base

75g (3oz, 6 tablespoons) unsalted butter

3 (4) tablespoons milk

15g (½ oz) fresh yeast

225g (8oz, 2 cups) strong plain flour

2 eggs, beaten

A pinch of salt

A pinch of brown sugar

ALTERNATIVE
CHEESE

Connoisseurs should look out for an
interesting English cheese called Stinking
Bishop. The rind is washed with the pear
variety of the same name, also used to
make perry or pear cider, which gives the
cheese its strong-smelling yet creamy-
tasting character

Like flamiche (see page 41), goyère is a rich cheese tart from Belgium and northern France. Some recipes specify a pastry base while others use a bread dough, similar to that of a pizza. Here I give my favourite version, which has a yeasted dough for the base. The filling for goyère is generally made with a pungent – or, frankly, smelly – rindwashed cheese such as Maroilles or Livarot. Not for the faint-hearted, but when mixed with smoked bacon and potatoes it makes a wonderfully flavoured dish.

For the base, warm the butter and milk over a low heat until the butter has just melted. Leave until tepid, then stir in the yeast until dissolved. Sift the flour into a bowl, make a well in the centre and add the beaten eggs, salt and brown sugar. Add the yeast mixture to the eggs and mix in the flour to give a smooth dough. Turn the dough out on to a lightly floured work surface and knead for 5 minutes or until smooth. Return it to the cleaned bowl, cover with a damp cloth and leave in a warm place until doubled in size.

For the filling, cook the potatoes in boiling salted water until just tender, then drain well. Heat the butter in a pan, add the onion and cook over a gentle heat until soft but not coloured. Add the bacon and cook for 5 minutes, then remove from the heat and leave to cool.

Put the potatoes, onion, bacon and cheese in a bowl and mix in the eggs and crème fraîche or cream. Season to taste with salt and pepper.

Knock back the risen dough and roll out until it is 5mm (¼ in) thick. Use to line a 23cm (9in) flan ring, leaving a good amount of dough overlapping the edge. Place on a baking sheet, fill with the potato, bacon and cheese mixture and leave in a warm place to rise for 30 minutes, until the dough is puffy. Preheat the oven to 170°C, 325°F, gas 3.

Trim off the excess dough, then bake the tart in the oven for 45 minutes– 1 hour, until golden and set.

Pear, Beenleigh Blue & Rosemary Galettes

SERVES 4

2 small egg whites

250g (9oz, generous 1 cup) Beenleigh Blue

1 tablespoon crème fraîche

1 quantity of shortcrust pastry (see page 21)

1 tablespoon finely chopped fresh rosemary, plus a few leaves to garnish

50g (2oz, 4 tablespoons) unsalted butter, plus a little melted butter for brushing

2 large, ripe but firm pears, peeled, cored & cut into slices 1cm (½ in) thick

1 tablespoon caster sugar

1 teaspoon cumin seeds

2 egg yolks, beaten with 1 tablespoon milk, to glaze

Salt & freshly ground black pepper

ALTERNATIVE
CHEESES

A fairly sharp blue cheese is needed, such as Gorgonzola or Roquefort

Ripe, sweet pears make an excellent foil for the sharp blue cheese and the aromatic rosemary. As an alternative dish, try replacing the pear and Beenleigh Blue with slices of mozzarella and tomato, top them with a covering of pesto and bake the galettes as usual.

Whisk the egg whites until just frothy. Put the cheese in a bowl and crush it lightly with a fork, then add the egg whites and crème fraîche and mix to a coarse paste. Season with salt and pepper, then chill.

Roll out the pastry to about 3mm (⅛ in) thick. Using a plain or fluted cutter, cut out four 12cm (5in) circles. Put them on a baking sheet and prick well all over with a fork to prevent them rising too much in the oven. Carefully spread the cheese mixture over the pastry rounds, leaving a 1–2cm (½–¾ in) border, then sprinkle with the chopped rosemary and place in the refrigerator.

Preheat the oven to 200°C, 400°F, gas 6. Melt the butter in a shallow pan, then add the pear slices, sugar and enough water to form a light syrup around the pears – about 3 (4) tablespoons. Cook gently for 6–8 minutes, until the pears are tender, then leave to cool.

Arrange the pear slices on top of the galettes in neatly overlapping circles and brush with a little melted butter. Sprinkle over the cumin seeds and a few rosemary leaves, season with salt and pepper and bring up the edges of the pastry over the pears to form a crust. Brush the pastry all over with the beaten egg yolks and bake for 15–20 minutes or until golden. Cool the galettes slightly before serving.

P.G.TIPS

The galettes can be assembled several hours in advance – or even the night before – and chilled until you are ready to bake them. If you prefer, you can substitute puff pastry for the shortcrust.

PEAR, BEENLEIGH BLUE
& ROSEMARY GALETTE

Warm Brioche of Goat's Cheese with Minted Leeks

SERVES 4

50g (2oz, 4 tablespoons) unsalted butter

2 young leeks, thinly sliced

1 tablespoon chopped fresh mint

Freshly grated nutmeg

4 brioche buns, 5cm (2in) in diameter
(see page 22)

4 crottin de Chavignol goat's cheeses, cut
horizontally in half

Salt & freshly ground black pepper

ALTERNATIVE
CHEESES

A good English alternative is a well-aged
Chabis, produced in East Sussex on the
same farm as Golden Cross. Or you could
use 4 slices of Sainte-Maure goat's cheese,
cut 2.5cm (1in) thick

I first prepared this brioche for a private party of eight vegetarians in the Lanesborough's Conservatory restaurant, as part of a seven-course gastronomic vegetarian menu. It was voted the star of the show and now makes regular appearances on my menu.

Preheat the oven to 200°C, 400°F, gas 6. Melt the butter in a pan, add the leeks and cook over a low heat for 8–10 minutes or until tender. You may need to add a little water if the leeks become too dry and stick to the pan. Remove from the pan and stir in the mint, then season to taste with nutmeg, salt and pepper.

Cut a 1cm (½ in) slice off the top of each brioche and set aside, then carefully hollow out the centre of each bun. Fill with the minted leeks. Top the leeks with the goat's cheese and then put the brioches in the oven for 5 minutes to heat through. The cheese should just be starting to melt. Replace the brioche tops and serve immediately.

P.G.TIPS

Try topping the cheese with a little basil pesto before putting the brioches in the oven. I much prefer to prepare fresh pesto, which can be made in minutes in a blender. Shop-bought pesto is fine, but nothing quite matches the flavour and aroma of fresh basil. Filo pastry makes a good substitute for the brioche: simply top the leeks with the cheese and wrap well in the filo, then bake until golden.

Flamiche aux Trois Fromages

SERVES 4–6

3 eggs

300ml (½ pint, 1¼ cups) double cream

100ml (3½ fl oz, ½ cup) milk

Freshly grated nutmeg

75g (3oz, scant ½ cup) Roquefort, cut into 1cm (½ in) cubes

75g (3oz, scant ½ cup) Emmenthal, grated

75g (3oz, scant ½ cup) Golden Cross, cut into 1cm (½ in) cubes

250g (9oz) puff pastry

Salt & freshly ground black pepper

ALTERNATIVE CHEESES

Any three varieties of cheese may be used, but I think a combination of goat's cheese, blue cheese and a hard cheese strikes the perfect balance

I first had this rich cheese tart at a simple country auberge in France some ten years ago, and its intense flavours have stayed in my mind to this day. The original recipe put Sainte-Maure goat's cheese with Roquefort and Emmenthal but I find the English goat's cheese, Golden Cross, a very worthy substitute. The cheeses are added to the pastry case separately rather than mixed together, so it's rather like a mini cheeseboard in a tart! This does mean, of course, that everyone is given a slightly different slice, which is fine if your guests all have individual preferences. Otherwise, lightly stir the cheese mixtures together to give a marbled effect.

Preheat the oven to 220°C, 425°F, gas 7. Beat together the eggs, cream and milk, seasoning them with nutmeg, salt and pepper. Divide equally between 3 bowls and stir a different cheese into each one. Leave to stand while you prepare the pastry.

Roll out the pastry thinly and use to line a 20–23cm (8–9in) tart tin. Prick the base all over with a fork to prevent it rising too much in the oven. Carefully pour the 3 cheese mixtures into 3 separate areas of the pastry case. Marble them lightly with a fork, if you like, or leave them separate. Bake for 30–40 minutes, until the tart is set and beautifully golden. Serve hot.

P.G. TIPS You could use shortcrust pastry (see page 21) instead of puff if you prefer, but you will need to bake the pastry case blind for 8–10 minutes before adding the filling. For a non-traditional but luxurious addition, spread 150g (5oz, 1 cup) fresh crabmeat over the pastry case before pouring in the filling.

Baked Reblochon in Savoy Cabbage

SERVES 4

3 (4) tablespoons vegetable oil

100g (4oz, ⅔ cup) potatoes, cut into 5mm (¼ in) cubes

1 onion, finely chopped

75g (3oz, ½ cup) smoked bacon, cut into *lardons* (small strips)

50g (2oz, 1 cup) chanterelle mushrooms, thinly sliced

75g (3oz, 1½ cups) button mushrooms, thinly sliced

2 tablespoons chopped fresh chives

8 green cabbage leaves, such as Savoy or Primo

Freshly grated nutmeg

1 Reblochon, rind removed

25g (1oz, 4 tablespoons) unsalted butter, melted

300ml (½ pint, 1¼ cups) Reduced Meat Stock (see page 17)

Salt & freshly ground black pepper

ALTERNATIVE
CHEESES

Baby Saint-Nectaire, Pont-l'Évêque or a plain or smoked Gubbeen

I got the idea for this recipe from Pierre Carrier, the proprietor of the Hotel Albert Premier in Chamonix, France. His version used a local Reblochon made of goat's milk, which is well worth buying if you ever happen to see it. Although the dish is fairly expensive to make, the flavours are out of this world. Serve as a substantial first course or a delicious and unusual lunch dish.

Heat 1 tablespoon of the oil in a frying pan and sauté the potatoes until golden brown and just tender. Remove from the pan and set aside. Add the remaining oil to the pan and stir in the onion, bacon and both types of mushroom. Raise the heat and cook until golden and tender. Add to the potatoes, stir in the chives and leave to cool.

Preheat the oven to 200°C, 400°F, gas 6. Trim the cabbage leaves and cook them in boiling salted water until just tender. Remove with a slotted spoon and refresh in cold running water, then drain well and dry on a cloth. Lay out the leaves, slightly overlapping, on a work surface and season with nutmeg, salt and pepper.

Slice the Reblochon in half horizontally, cover one half with the potato mixture and top with the other half to form a sandwich. Place the Reblochon in the centre of the cabbage leaves and fold them over to cover the cheese completely. Season again and brush with the melted butter. Place in a baking dish and bake for about 12–15 minutes, until thoroughly heated through. Meanwhile, heat the reduced meat stock. When ready, transfer the cheese to a serving dish and pour the meat stock around it. Serve cut into wedges.

P.G.TIPS

Try wrapping the cheese in puff pastry rather than cabbage leaves. Swiss chard or spinach could easily replace the cabbage, if preferred. For vegetarians, the meat stock can be substituted with red wine vinegar or walnut oil dressing.

Greek-style Baked Artichokes with Coriander, Mint & Lemon

8 medium or 4 large globe artichokes
Juice & zest of 1 lemon
50g (2oz, 1 cup) fresh white breadcrumbs
2 garlic cloves, crushed
1 tablespoon chopped fresh mint
1 tablespoon chopped fresh coriander
50g (2oz, ½ cup) kasseri, grated
150ml (¼ pint, ⅔ cup) olive oil
75g (3oz, scant ½ cup) feta, crumbled
150ml (¼ pint, ⅔ cup) dry white wine
Salt & freshly ground black pepper

ALTERNATIVE CHEESES

There is an American version of kasseri from Wisconsin, made with cow's milk and tasting a little sharper and saltier. Italian provolone could be used instead

You need kasseri cheese for this recipe, a mild, creamy sheep's milk cheese which is now available from some Greek delicatessens. The artichokes are filled with a tangy cheese and herb mixture, which also makes a very good stuffing for tomatoes and aubergines.

Preheat the oven to 180°C, 350°F, gas 4. To prepare the artichokes, snap off the stalks and trim away the dark, fibrous outer leaves until you reach the tender, inner green leaves, rubbing the artichokes with the lemon juice as you go to prevent discoloration. Slice off about one third from the top of each artichoke. Carefully remove the hairy inner choke with a teaspoon. Drop the artichokes into a bowl of water acidulated with lemon juice.

In a bowl, mix together the lemon zest, breadcrumbs, garlic, mint, coriander, grated kasseri and 2 tablespoons of the olive oil. Season with salt and pepper.

Drain and dry the artichokes, then fill them with the feta. Top with the stuffing mixture. Place them in a baking dish, sprinkle over the white wine and the remaining oil and top up with water until the liquid reaches halfway up the sides of the artichokes. Bake for 35 minutes or until tender, basting frequently, then put the artichokes under a hot grill for a few minutes to brown the stuffing. Serve hot or cold.

Crisp, Flowering Courgettes with Mozzarella & Anchovy

SERVES 4

8 courgettes, about 5cm (2in) long, with
flowers still attached

4 canned anchovy fillets

1 ball of cow's milk mozzarella

3 (4) tablespoons Chinese flour (see Tip)

Vegetable oil for deep-frying

Salt & freshly ground black pepper

Sprigs of fresh flat-leaf parsley, to garnish

Lemon wedges, to serve

My good friend Stuart Partridge, chef at the Hassler Hotel in Rome, first prepared this dish during a recent visit to the Lanesborough. I love the pure simplicity of its flavours. You could serve the courgettes with a tomato sauce but I like them best with just a squeeze of lemon juice. Although very young courgettes with their yellow flowers still attached are sold in markets in France and Italy, they are not generally available in the UK. However, if you grow your own courgettes, you can pick them for this recipe when they are just the right size.

Trim about 1cm (½in) off the end of each courgette and discard (or save for another use). Carefully wipe clean the courgette flowers and remove the stamen from the centre of each one. Soak the anchovy fillets in water for 10 minutes, then dry them on kitchen paper. Cut each anchovy fillet in half. Cut the mozzarella into 8 batons approximately the size of your index finger. Place a piece of anchovy on each mozzarella baton, then place inside the courgette flowers and twist the ends of the blossoms to secure the filling.

Mix the Chinese flour with enough water to make a thin batter; it should coat the back of a spoon. Heat the oil in a deep-fat fryer or large saucepan to 180°C, 350°F. Dip the stuffed courgettes in the batter and deep-fry them for 1–2 minutes, until crisp and golden, turning them occasionally. Drain them thoroughly on kitchen paper. Quickly drop the sprigs of parsley into the hot oil and fry for about 10 seconds, until crisp, then drain on kitchen paper. Serve the courgettes immediately, garnished with the deep-fried parsley and accompanied by lemon wedges.

P.G.TIPS

Chinese flour is available in oriental food shops, but if you can't find any, make a tempura batter instead. Put 1 small egg yolk and 125ml (4fl oz, ½ cup) iced water in a bowl, then gently mix in 125g (4½ oz, 1 cup) plain flour and a pinch of salt; it should be slightly lumpy. Dip the stuffed courgettes in the batter and proceed as above. If you are keen to try this recipe but can't track down courgette flowers, wrap the cheese and anchovy in blanched spinach or roll in sautéed thin slices of aubergine before frying.

Melting Camembert Fritters on Gooseberry & Green Peppercorn Chutney

SERVES 4–6

350g (12oz, 1½ cups) Camembert, not too ripe

50g (2oz, 4 tablespoons) unsalted butter

50g (2oz, ½ cup) plain flour, plus extra for coating

350ml (12 fl oz, 1½ cups) milk, boiled & strained

3 egg yolks

1 teaspoon Dijon mustard

Freshly grated nutmeg

1 egg, beaten

100g (4oz, 2 cups) white breadcrumbs

Vegetable oil for deep-frying

4 (5) good tablespoons Gooseberry & Green Peppercorn Chutney (see page 186)

Salt & freshly ground black pepper

ALTERNATIVE
CHEESES

Irish Cooleeney, Scottish Bonchester, Welsh Pencarreg or Sharpham

Don't expect these fritters to be anything like those breaded wedges of Camembert, deep-fried and served with a cloyingly sweet jam, that enjoyed inexplicable popularity on restaurant menus in the Seventies and Eighties. Here, the fritters are made with a thick, well-flavoured cheese sauce that has little cubes of Camembert stirred in to give a wonderful melting contrast. The accompanying chutney is refreshingly tart.

Remove the rind from the Camembert and cut the cheese into small pieces. Melt the butter in a pan over a low heat, stir in the flour and cook for 2–3 minutes. Gradually add the boiled milk, stirring all the time, then bring to the boil and simmer gently for 5–10 minutes to give a thick sauce. Remove from the heat, add half the Camembert and allow the cheese to melt in the sauce. Cool slightly, then beat in the egg yolks one at a time. Stir in the mustard and season with nutmeg, salt and pepper, then stir in the remaining cheese. Pour into a greased shallow dish or a small Swiss roll tin. The mixture should be about 2cm (¾ in) deep. Leave to cool, then cover and chill for at least 4 hours, preferably overnight.

Remove the cheese mixture from the refrigerator and, using a 5cm (2in) cutter, cut out 12 circles. Coat them lightly in flour, dip in the beaten egg and then in the breadcrumbs.

Heat the oil in a deep-fat fryer or a large saucepan to 180°C, 350°F, then fry the fritters a few at a time for 3–4 minutes, until golden. Drain on kitchen paper and serve immediately, accompanied by the chutney.

Carpaccio of Beef with Dolcelatte Mustard Dressing

SERVES 4

450g (1lb) beef fillet

4 (5) tablespoons olive oil

2 tablespoons coarse sea salt

300g (11oz) celeriac

Juice of ½ lemon

3 (4) tablespoons walnut oil

225g (8oz) cornsalad (or mixed salad leaves)

Salt & freshly ground black pepper

For the dressing

1 egg yolk

2 tablespoons Dijon mustard

1 tablespoon white wine vinegar

1 teaspoon soft brown sugar

5 (6) tablespoons vegetable oil

1 tablespoon finely chopped fresh dill, plus a few sprigs to garnish

50g (2oz, ¼ cup) dolcelatte

ALTERNATIVE
CHEESES

Dunsyre Blue, Danish Blue, Blue Castello (Aust) or Unity Blue (Aust)

This mustard and blue cheese dressing makes a good alternative to the olive oil and Parmesan cheese that normally accompany carpaccio of beef. To make a warm carpaccio, use thin steaks – about 5mm (¼in) thick – and grill over a charcoal grill for about 1 minute per side.

Cut the beef fillet into wafer-thin slices across the grain. If you find it difficult to slice the meat this thinly, cut thicker slices, place them between 2 sheets of oiled cling film and beat out carefully with a rolling pin or meat mallet. Spread the slices in a single layer over 4 large serving plates. Sprinkle with the olive oil, coarse salt and some freshly ground black pepper.

For the dressing, put the egg yolk in a bowl and whisk in the mustard, vinegar and sugar. Gradually add the oil in a thin stream, whisking all the time, as if making mayonnaise. Stir in the chopped dill. Put the dolcelatte in a separate bowl, pour on 2 tablespoons of boiling water and mix to a smooth paste. Add this paste to the dressing, blending it in well. Adjust the seasoning carefully as the dolcelatte will be quite salty.

Peel the celeriac, then grate it coarsely or cut it into fine strips (a mandolin is useful for this). Put it in a bowl, toss with the lemon juice and walnut oil and season to taste.

To serve, toss the cornsalad with the dressing and arrange on top of the beef, then sprinkle over the celeriac. Garnish with sprigs of dill.

P.G. TIPS

Chill the beef briefly in the freezer to make it easier to slice. If the prospect of slicing and salting the beef seems daunting, try using a cured meat such as Bresaola or even Parma ham – they both work well. The crisp, nutty texture of the celeriac lends a special flavour to the dish. Make every effort to get hold of some; you will not be disappointed!

Chapter Two

SOUPS

Pear, Celeriac & Stilton Vichysoisse

SERVES 4

25g (1oz, 2 tablespoons) unsalted butter
1 onion, finely diced
300g (11oz) celeriac, peeled & finely diced
2 ripe pears, peeled, cored & finely diced
1 litre (1¾ pints, 4 cups) Chicken Stock
(see page 16) or Vegetable Stock
(see page 16)
750ml (1¼ pints, 3 cups) single cream
75g (3oz, scant ½ cup) Stilton, crumbled
2 tablespoons chopped fresh chives
Salt & freshly ground black pepper

ALTERNATIVE
CHEESES

Shropshire Blue, dolcelatte, Milawa Blue
(Aust), Gippsland Tarago River Blue
(Aust) or Oregon Blue (US)

Some people are quite purist about what should go in a vichysoisse, which traditionally is made with leek and potato, but I think this version is definitely worthy of consideration. Intense yet delicate in flavour, it makes an ideal soup for early autumn. Like the original, it's thickened with cream and served chilled, garnished with chives.

Heat the butter in a pan, add the onion and celeriac and cook over a gentle heat until they begin to soften, about 8–10 minutes. Stir in the pears and cook for 3–4 minutes. Add the stock and bring to the boil, then reduce the heat and simmer for 25 minutes, until the vegetables are tender. Remove from the heat, stir in the cream and Stilton and then purée the soup in a blender until smooth. Leave to cool, then chill thoroughly.

Before serving it may be necessary to thin down the soup with a little milk, stock or cream. Stir in the chives and season to taste.

P.G.TIPS

I'm often asked what is the correct consistency for puréed soups. In my experience, a good general rule is that they should be approximately the consistency of single cream, that is thick enough to coat the back of a spoon.

Pea & Watercress Soup with Emmenthal Floating Islands

SERVES 4

50g (2oz, 4 tablespoons) unsalted butter

50g (2oz, ½ cup) onion, roughly chopped

1 leek, roughly chopped

1 litre (1¾ pints, 4 cups) Chicken Stock (see page 16)

450g (1lb, 4 cups) shelled fresh or frozen peas

2 bunches of watercress, tough stalks removed

2 egg whites

75g (3oz, ¾ cup) Emmenthal cheese, freshly grated, plus extra to serve

600ml (1 pint, 2½ cups) milk

150ml (¼ pint, ⅔ cup) double cream

Salt & freshly ground black pepper

These cloud-like cheese meringues not only taste great but also make a lovely presentation for this delicate, peppery-tasting pea soup.

Heat the butter in a heavy-based pan, add the onion and leek and cook gently for 4–5 minutes, until softened. Add the stock and bring to the boil. Add the peas and simmer until tender – the cooking time will depend on whether you are using fresh or frozen peas. Stir in the watercress, then pour the soup into a blender and blitz until very smooth. For a more refined finish, strain it through a fine sieve afterwards.

Whisk the egg whites until they form stiff peaks and gently fold in the grated cheese. Use 2 tablespoons to shape the mixture into *quenelles*: to do this, take a tablespoonful of the mixture and then shape it with the second spoon, turning it between the two. Or you can just scoop it into 8–12 balls. Bring the milk to a simmer in a large pan. Poach the *quenelles* in it for 3–4 minutes, until set, turning them over halfway through. Remove with a slotted spoon and drain well.

Add the cream to the soup and reheat without letting it boil, then season to taste. Pour into warm bowls and serve topped with the cheese meringues and some shavings of Emmenthal.

P.G.TIPS

You could poach the floating islands in water, but they have a better flavour if you use milk. Save the milk afterwards to make a cheese sauce, if you like.

Potato & Cantal Soup

SERVES 4

50g (2oz, 4 tablespoons) unsalted butter

600g (1lb 6oz) potatoes, cut into slices 1cm (½ in) thick

250g (9oz) leeks, white part only, finely sliced

3 garlic cloves, crushed

600ml (1 pint, 2½ cups) Chicken Stock (see page 16) or Vegetable Stock (see page 16)

90ml (3 fl oz, ⅓ cup) double cream

300ml (½ pint, 1¼ cups) milk, boiled & strained

175g (6oz, 1½ cups) mature Cantal, grated

Salt & freshly ground black pepper

ALTERNATIVE

CHEESES

Beaufort, Gruyère or Emmenthal

Sometimes known as French Cheddar, Cantal is a very versatile cooking cheese and is particularly good in soups, sauces and gratins. It is at its best in late summer, when the milk is at its richest. Winter vegetables such as cabbage and carrots are often added to this soup along with the potatoes. I like to serve it with thin slices of toasted baguette rubbed with oil and garlic.

Heat the butter in a large saucepan, add the potatoes, leeks and garlic, then cover and sweat for 4–5 minutes. Pour in the stock and bring to the boil. Skim to remove any impurities from the surface, reduce the heat and simmer until the vegetables are just cooked. Add the cream and boiled milk and heat through gently, then stir in the grated Cantal. Remove from the heat, season to taste and serve.

Zuppa Pavese

SERVES 4

6 fresh eggs

8 slices of white country-style bread, cut 1cm (½ in) thick

100g (4oz, 1 cup) Parmesan, grated

50g (2oz, 4 tablespoons) unsalted butter

1 litre (1¾ pints, 4 cups) Meat Stock (see page 17) or, better still, consommé

Salt & freshly ground black pepper

This rustic Italian soup is very nourishing and quick and easy to make. All you do is pour a well-flavoured broth over slices of fried bread and then slip in an egg, which cooks in the heat of the broth. However, such simplicity relies on the finest ingredients for its success: don't make the soup unless you have homemade stock, good country-style bread and free-range eggs.

Beat 2 of the eggs in a bowl, season lightly, then pour them into a shallow dish. Dip the bread slices in the beaten egg on both sides, then dredge them in 75g (3oz, ¾ cup) of the grated Parmesan. Heat the butter in a large frying pan and fry the bread until golden on both sides.

Put the slices of fried bread in 4 deep, heatproof serving bowls. Bring the stock or consommé to the boil and pour it over the bread to immerse it completely. Crack an egg into each bowl on top of the bread. Leave the bowls on the side of the stove or over a very low heat to allow the eggs to cook lightly. Serve with the remaining cheese on the side, for sprinkling over the soup.

P.G.TIPS
If you prefer, you can poach the eggs in the hot stock in a saucepan, then place them on the fried bread in the soup bowls and pour the soup over.

White Cabbage & Oyster Broth with Fourme d'Ambert Cheese

SERVES 4

50g (2oz, 4 tablespoons) unsalted butter

200g (7oz) white cabbage, cut into 2cm (¾ in) dice

1 teaspoon cumin seeds

1 litre (1¾ pints, 4 cups) Vegetable Stock (see page 16) or Chicken Stock (see page 16)

12 fresh oysters

50g (2oz, ¼ cup) Fourme d'Ambert

5 (6) tablespoons double cream

1 tablespoon chopped fresh chives (optional)

Salt & freshly ground black pepper

ALTERNATIVE

CHEESES

Dunsyre Blue or Cashel Blue

This soup dates back to my early days at Inigo Jones restaurant in London's Covent Garden. I enjoy preparing and tasting it as much now as I did then. You can make the soup without the oysters and it's still good, but they do give it an incomparable briny scent and flavour.

Melt the butter in a saucepan, add the cabbage, then cover and sweat for 5–8 minutes. Stir in the cumin seeds, pour in the stock and bring to the boil. Skim off any impurities that rise to the surface and simmer gently for about 15 minutes, until the cabbage is tender.

Meanwhile, open the oyster shells and remove the oysters, reserving their juice (see Tip on page 30). Cut the oysters in half and strain the juice through a piece of muslin. Set aside.

Pass the Fourme d'Ambert cheese through a fine sieve and blend it with the cream. Stir the cream into the soup and adjust the seasoning. Add the cleaned oysters together with their strained juice, sprinkle with the chives, if using, and serve immediately.

P.G. TIPS

On no account let the soup boil after the cheese and cream mixture has been added to it or the delicate flavour will be spoiled. If the briny taste of oysters is not to your liking, you may prefer to substitute mussels. Simply cook the mussels with a little water until they open, then strain the cooking juices into the soup.

Cannellini Bean Soup with Fontina Gremolata

SERVES 4

50g (2oz, 4 tablespoons) unsalted butter

75g (3oz, ½ cup) onions, diced

1 garlic clove, crushed

200g (7oz, generous 1 cup) cannellini beans, soaked overnight & then drained

50g (2oz, ¼ cup) carrot, diced

½ red chilli, deseeded & finely chopped

2 ripe tomatoes, chopped

2 cardamom pods, crushed

1 teaspoon cumin seeds

1.3 litres (2¼ pints, 5¾ cups) Chicken Stock (see page 16) or Vegetable Stock (see page 16)

Salt & freshly ground black pepper

For the gremolata

75g (3oz, ¾ cup) fontina, very finely grated

1 tablespoon finely grated lemon zest

1 tablespoon fresh thyme leaves

2 garlic cloves, crushed

ALTERNATIVE CHEESES

Raclette, Taleggio or Port Salut

A heartwarming, lightly spiced soup topped with stringy fontina cheese and spiked with lemon. Serve with chunks of fresh bread.

Melt the butter in a pan over a medium heat, add the onions and garlic and sauté for 4–5 minutes, until softened. Add the cannellini beans, carrot, chilli and tomatoes, then cover and cook gently for 5 minutes. Next, stir in the cardamom, cumin seeds and stock and bring to the boil. Reduce the heat and simmer for 1–1½ hours, or until the beans are tender. Pour the soup into a blender and blitz to a purée, then strain it through a fine sieve to give a creamy texture. Adjust the seasoning and reheat gently.

For the gremolata, mix all the ingredients together in a bowl. Pour the soup into warm bowls, scatter with the gremolata and serve straight away.

P.G. TIPS

Other pulses such as lentils can be used with just as good effect. I sometimes leave the beans whole and top them with the gremolata to serve as a winter stew.

Tomato Gazpacho with Cabécou-stuffed Tomatoes

SERVES 4

900g (2lb) overripe plum tomatoes (or use half plum tomatoes, half beef tomatoes)

1 tablespoon tomato ketchup

1 tablespoon olive oil

1 small garlic clove, peeled

1 tablespoon caster sugar

150ml (¼ pint, ⅔ cup) Vegetable Stock (see page 16)

A bunch of fresh basil

2 tablespoons red wine vinegar

2 tablespoons dry vermouth

Salt & freshly ground white pepper

For the stuffed tomatoes

2 Cabécou cheeses or other small, firm goat's cheeses

½ onion, very finely chopped

1 small courgette, very finely chopped

1 egg yolk

25g (1oz, ½ cup) mixed fresh herbs, such as basil, chervil, parsley & chives, finely chopped

2–3 (4) tablespoons fresh white breadcrumbs

8 ripe but firm small tomatoes

A little olive oil for brushing

The surprising thing about this recipe is the stunning contrast of hot and cold. The chilled smooth gazpacho is poured around stuffed tomatoes that have come straight from the oven. The soup is strongly scented with basil, which I love to use in large quantities, but you can always reduce the amount if you prefer or if you don't have much available.

For the soup, blanch the tomatoes in boiling water for 1 minute, then drain and refresh in ice-cold water. Drain again and peel. Cut the tomatoes in half and put them in a bowl with the tomato ketchup, olive oil, garlic, sugar, vegetable stock and leaves from the bunch of basil, reserving 8–12 leaves for garnishing the finished dish. Stir in the red wine vinegar and vermouth, season lightly and leave to marinate for 1–2 hours.

Strain the tomato mixture through a fine sieve into a bowl, pushing hard to extract all the juice (don't use a blender or the fresh colour of the tomatoes will be lost). Adjust the seasoning, then chill until ready to serve.

For the stuffed tomatoes, preheat the oven to 180°C, 350°F, gas 4. Put the goat's cheese in a bowl and crush with a fork. Stir in the onion, courgette, egg yolk and herbs, then add enough breadcrumbs to bind the mixture lightly together. Season to taste. Slice a lid off the top of each tomato and reserve. Carefully scoop out the pulp and seeds from the tomatoes with a spoon. Fill them with the stuffing, brush with a little olive oil and bake for 5 minutes, until soft and heated through.

Place 2 stuffed tomatoes in each soup plate and replace their lids, then carefully pour the gazpacho around. Decorate with the reserved basil leaves and serve immediately.

P.G.TIPS

Make this soup in late summer when overripe tomatoes are being sold off cheaply. I strongly recommend that you keep this delicate, fresh-tasting soup for the summer months, as tomatoes have less flavour, juice and sweetness in winter.

Cauliflower Cheese Soup

SERVES 4

1 large cauliflower, weighing about 750g (1lb 10oz)

50g (2oz, 4 tablespoons) unsalted butter

1 onion, thinly sliced

1 leek, thinly sliced

1 litre (1¾ pints, 4 cups) Vegetable Stock (see page 16) or water

2 egg yolks

4 (5) tablespoons double cream

75g (3oz, ¾ cup) farmhouse Cheddar, grated

Freshly grated nutmeg

Salt & freshly ground black pepper

ALTERNATIVE
CHEESES

A soft goat's cheese or Stilton

According to a recent survey, by far the most popular vegetable dish in the UK is cauliflower cheese. Let's face it, it's something we all enjoy. So why not try cauliflower cheese soup?

Trim the outer green leaves off the cauliflower and cut it into florets. Heat the butter in a heavy-based saucepan, add the onion and leek, then cover and cook gently for 2–3 minutes, until the vegetables begin to soften. Do not let them brown. Add the cauliflower florets (reserving a few small ones as a garnish) and cook gently for 4–5 minutes. Pour in the stock or water, bring to the boil, then reduce the heat and simmer for 20–25 minutes, until the cauliflower is very tender. Meanwhile, cook the reserved cauliflower florets in boiling salted water until just tender. Drain, refresh in cold water, then drain again well and reserve.

Purée the soup in a blender until smooth, return it to the saucepan and bring to the boil. In a bowl, lightly whisk together the egg yolks, cream and cheese. Whisk about 6 (8) tablespoons of the soup into this mixture, then stir it back into the remainder of the soup; do not let it boil. Season with nutmeg, salt and pepper, then serve garnished with the cooked cauliflower florets.

Kohlrabi & Gorgonzola Soup

SERVES 4

25g (1oz, 2 tablespoons) unsalted butter

2 kohlrabi, peeled & cut into small cubes

1 potato, peeled & cut into small cubes

1 litre (1¾ pints, 4 cups) Chicken Stock
(see page 16)

100ml (3½ fl oz, ½ cup) milk

100ml (3½ fl oz, ½ cup) double cream

75g (3oz, scant ½ cup) Gorgonzola,
crumbled

Salt & freshly ground black pepper

ALTERNATIVE
CHEESES

Fourme d'Ambert, Gippsland Blue (Aust)
or Milawa Blue (Aust)

Kohlrabi is a strange and, in my view, much underrated vegetable. It looks like a turnip but is in fact a member of the cabbage family. Its mild flavour is very good with Gorgonzola; however if you can't find kohlrabi, you could substitute sweet potatoes, turnips or cauliflower.

Heat the butter in a pan, add the kohlrabi and potato and cook over a gentle heat for 2–3 minutes. Add the stock and bring to the boil, then reduce the heat and simmer for 20–25 minutes, until the vegetables are very soft. Purée the soup in a blender until smooth. Pour it back into the pan, add the milk and cream and bring to the boil. Remove from the heat and stir in the Gorgonzola. Season to taste and serve.

Lobster & Gospel Green Cheddar Bisque

SERVES 4

1 cooked lobster, weighing about 750g (1lb 10oz)

75g (3oz, 6 tablespoons) unsalted butter

½ onion, roughly chopped

1 celery stick, roughly chopped

1 carrot, roughly chopped

2 garlic cloves, crushed

2 tablespoons tomato purée

4 (5) tablespoons cognac

150ml (¼ pint, ⅔ cup) dry white wine

1 tablespoon fresh tarragon leaves, plus a few sprigs to garnish

75g (3oz, ¾ cup) plain flour

1 litre (1¾ pints, 4 cups) Chicken Stock (see page 16)

150ml (¼ pint, ⅔ cup) double cream

75g (3oz, ¾ cup) Gospel Green Cheddar, grated

Cayenne pepper

Salt & freshly ground black pepper

Gospel Green is a superb unpasteurized farmhouse Cheddar made in Surrey. It's worth seeking out, although you can of course substitute any other farmhouse Cheddar in this recipe. The bisque is also very good made with crab or langoustines instead of lobster.

Split the lobster in half down the back: the easiest way to do this is to put a large knife through the centre of the body section and cut down through the head, then take out the knife, turn the lobster round and cut down the centre of the body through the tail. Remove and discard the head sac and the intestinal vein, then remove the cooked lobster flesh from the head and tail. Crack the claws in 2 or 3 places and pick out the meat. Place the lobster shells in a bowl and, using a meat hammer, crush them into smallish pieces. This helps to extract maximum flavour.

Heat the butter in a heavy-based pan, add the crushed lobster shells and fry for 4–5 minutes, until they begin to turn golden. Add the vegetables and garlic and fry for 5 minutes, until softened. Stir in the tomato purée, then add the cognac, white wine and tarragon leaves and cook for 5 minutes. Stir in the flour and cook for a further 5 minutes. Add the stock, bring to the boil and skim off any impurities that rise to the surface. Reduce the heat and simmer for 30–40 minutes.

Meanwhile, dice the lobster flesh and set aside. Bring the cream to the boil in a separate pan, then remove from the heat. Add the cheese and stir until melted and smooth, then set aside.

Blitz the soup in a blender until the shells are quite finely ground, then pass it through a very fine sieve and stir in the cheese cream. Add cayenne, salt and pepper to taste, then pour the soup into warm bowls. Garnish with the diced lobster and sprigs of tarragon, dust very lightly with cayenne and serve.

P.G. TIPS

Rice may be used instead of flour to thicken the soup. It is important that you do not cook the stock for longer than 40 minutes, as it will lose its natural flavours and become bitter. If you decide to use crab instead of lobster, cook the live crabs for 12–15 minutes, depending on their size.

Bread & Pecorino Soup

SERVES 4

1 litre (1¾ pints, 4 cups) Chicken Stock
(see page 16)

4 (5) tablespoons olive oil

2 garlic cloves, crushed

275g (10oz, 1⅔ cups) potatoes, peeled &
cut into small cubes

4 thick slices of stale Italian country
bread, cut into cubes

6 (8) tablespoons grated pecorino

1 tablespoon coarsely chopped fresh
marjoram

¼ teaspoon grated lemon zest

Salt

Cracked black pepper (see Tip on
page 146)

Like Zuppa Pavese (see page 54), this is an Italian peasant-style soup. I love the simplicity of it, made with just a few basic ingredients and a little care. It makes thrifty use of leftovers but it is essential to have good-quality stock. Good-quality olive oil is also a must, and you should not neglect the lemon; however strange it may sound, it really does give a little lift to this heart-warming one-pot soup.

Bring the stock to the boil with 3 (4) tablespoons of the olive oil, add the garlic and potatoes and return to the boil. Add the bread cubes and simmer for 20–25 minutes, until the potatoes are tender.

Remove the pan from the heat and stir in the pecorino, marjoram and lemon zest. Season with a little salt and a sprinkling of freshly cracked black pepper. Drizzle over the remaining olive oil and serve straight away.

French Onion Soup with Beer & Camembert

SERVES 4

75g (3oz, 6 tablespoons) unsalted butter

300g (11oz, 3 cups) onions, finely sliced

½ tablespoon sugar

1 tablespoon plain flour

1 teaspoon tomato purée

100ml (3½ fl oz, ½ cup) light beer

1 litre (1¾ pints, 4 cups) Meat Stock
(see page 17)

1 ficelle (small, thin baguette) or 2 crusty
bread rolls, thinly sliced & toasted

100g (4oz, ½ cup) Camembert, rind
removed, thinly sliced

Salt & freshly ground black pepper

ALTERNATIVE

CHEESES

Carré de l'Est,

This variation on the classic French onion soup replaces the usual white wine and Gruyère with ingredients from Normandy – beer and Camembert cheese. I have successfully replaced the Camembert with Carré de l'Est, which is milder in flavour and has a delicate aroma when ripe. You can, of course, use grated Gruyère or Emmenthal for a more traditional onion soup.

Heat the butter in a heavy-based pan, add the onions and sugar and cook over a medium heat for at least 20 minutes, until very soft, golden and caramelized. Stir in the flour and tomato purée and cook for 2 minutes, until they brown very slightly. Pour in the beer, bring to the boil and after 1 minute add the stock. Reduce the heat and simmer for 15–20 minutes, then season to taste.

Pour the soup into 4 heatproof soup bowls or 1 large tureen and float the toasted bread on top in a single layer. Cover this with the Camembert slices. Put the bowls under a hot grill (or in a hot oven) until the cheese forms a well-browned crust. Serve immediately.

Saffron Vegetable Chowder with Coriander & Goat's Cheese Pesto

SERVES 4

3 (4) tablespoons olive oil

1 garlic clove, crushed

1 leek, 1 carrot, 1 celery stick, 1 courgette,
1 potato, all cut into 5mm (¼ in) dice

1 litre (1¾ pints, 4 cups) Vegetable Stock
(see page 16) or Chicken Stock
(see page 16)

A pinch of saffron strands

2 tomatoes, skinned, deseeded & cut into
5mm (¼ in) dice

2 tablespoons Coriander & Goat's Cheese
Pesto (see page 20)

125ml (4 fl oz, ½ cup) milk

Salt & freshly ground black pepper

A beautifully delicate vegetable chowder spiked with aromatic saffron and coriander. Saffron is now much more readily available, and imports from Spain and the Middle East continue to improve. It is an expensive spice but it has no substitute, especially in this chowder. Sachets of powdered saffron are cheaper than saffron strands but they cannot compete with them in flavour – always buy the real thing.

Heat the olive oil in a heavy-based pan, together with the garlic. Next, add the leek, carrot, celery, courgette and potato and cook for 2 minutes over a low heat.

Add the stock and saffron and bring to the boil. Reduce the heat and simmer for 20–25 minutes, until the vegetables are tender. Add the tomatoes and pesto and stir thoroughly, then add the milk. Season to taste with salt and pepper and serve immediately.

P.G.TIPS

As an effective variation, replace the coriander and goat's cheese pesto with fresh herbs, such as parsley, basil or chives.

Chapter Three

SALADS

Plum Tomato Salad with Goat's Milk Dressing

SERVES 4

8 large, ripe but firm plum tomatoes, cut into slices 5mm (¼ in) thick

75g (3oz, scant ½ cup) Roubiliac or Golden Cross goat's cheese

90ml (3 fl oz, ⅓ cup) goat's milk

2 tablespoons Greek yoghurt

1 tablespoon chopped fresh basil

1 tablespoon chopped fresh oregano

½ tablespoon chopped fresh coriander

Salt & freshly ground black pepper

The simplest of tomato salads, topped with a creamy dressing made with goat's cheese and goat's milk. Serve as an accompaniment or as part of a selection of salads for a picnic.

Arrange the tomato slices in overlapping circles in a shallow serving bowl. Season with salt and pepper. Whisk all the remaining ingredients together and pour over the tomatoes. Serve well chilled.

P.G.TIPS

If you can't find goat's milk, cow's milk works well, too. I personally see no gain in removing the tomato skins for this salad, especially in summer when tomatoes are at their best. It is, of course, a matter of choice, and others may like to blanch them briefly in boiling water before peeling off the skins. Chives, parsley or chervil would make excellent alternative herbs, but they must be fresh.

Blackened Leek, Red Onion & Smoked Mozzarella Salad with Tarragon Vinaigrette

A pinch of sugar

24 young leeks, trimmed

2 red onions, cut into wedges

1 smoked mozzarella cheese, cut into 8 thin slices

Salt & freshly ground black pepper

For the vinaigrette

3 (4) tablespoons tarragon vinegar or champagne vinegar

1 teaspoon Dijon mustard

1 tablespoon chopped fresh tarragon

135ml (4½ fl oz, generous ½ cup) extra-virgin olive oil

1 tomato, deseeded & finely diced

1 tablespoon superfine capers, rinsed & drained

1 tablespoon green olives, stoned & finely chopped

1 hard-boiled egg, chopped

ALTERNATIVE
CHEESES

Buffalo mozzarella or a goat's cheese, such as coarsely grated crottin

I love the smoky flavours that predominate in this salad. The tart vinaigrette makes an ideal dressing for the charred leeks. If possible, cook the vegetables on a barbecue.

Bring a large pan of water to the boil with the sugar and a little salt. Throw in the leeks, return to the boil and cook gently for 2–3 minutes. Drain them well and dry on a cloth.

For the vinaigrette, mix the vinegar, mustard and tarragon together in a bowl and then whisk in the olive oil. Add all the remaining ingredients and season to taste with salt and pepper.

Grill the leeks and onions – for the best flavour this should be done on a barbecue or a ridged cast-iron grill pan, but you can also cook them under a preheated grill. When they are tender and slightly blackened, remove from the heat and season with salt and pepper.

Toss the leeks and onions with the vinaigrette and adjust the seasoning. Arrange on 4 serving plates, drape 2 slices of mozzarella over each portion and serve.

P.G.TIPS

Smoked mozzarella may not be a recognised household cheese, yet for me it is one of the nicest smoked cheeses. It is worth seeking out but, if you have a problem finding it, a creamy-tasting natural mozzarella would be fine.

Warm Lentil Salad with Pepper-grilled Goat's Cheese & Anchovy Toasts

*T*he dark greeny-blue French lentilles du Puy *are generally considered to have the best flavour and are well worth buying. They have recently been granted* appellation d'origine contrôlée *status, just like a fine wine or cheese, which means that only lentils from a particular corner of France – the area around Puy-en-Velay in the Haute Loire – are entitled to be called Puy. This decree is causing consternation among some British supermarket chains, which sell 'Puy lentils' that have in fact been produced in Canada. If you can't get the genuine article, don't worry! Cannellini beans also work very well in this winter salad.*

Put the lentils in a saucepan, cover with cold water and bring to the boil, skimming off any impurities that rise to the surface. Add the onion and cumin seeds and simmer for 30–40 minutes, until the lentils are just tender. Drain them well. Mix the olive oil, vinegar and shallot together and stir into the lentils. Keep warm.

For the cheese and anchovy toasts, work the anchovies and egg yolk to a paste with a pestle and mortar, then gradually blend in the olive oil to give a thick purée. Toast the French bread and spread with the anchovy paste, then top each one with 2 pieces of goat's cheese. Sprinkle over the thyme or rosemary leaves and black pepper and place under a hot grill until lightly browned. Put the warm lentils on serving plates, top with the toasts and serve straight away.

P.G.TIPS **Because the quantities for the anchovy paste are small, you really need to use a pestle and mortar. However, if you double the amount, you can blitz everything together in a blender. You are bound to find a use for the surplus; store it in the refrigerator and toss with pasta or use in sandwiches.**

Spinach, Blue Cheese & Avocado Salad with Pumpkin Seeds

SERVES 4

350g (12oz) tender young spinach leaves

100g (4oz, 2 cups) mushrooms, sliced

2 hard-boiled eggs, chopped

75g (3oz, scant ½ cup) blue cheese, in 1cm (½ in) cubes

1 garlic clove, crushed

200g (7oz, scant 1 cup) fromage frais

1 teaspoon mild Dijon mustard

1 teaspoon lemon juice

1 avocado, peeled, stoned & cut into 1cm (½ in) cubes

12 slices of small baguette, toasted

50g (2oz, ½ cup) pumpkin seeds, toasted

Salt & freshly ground black pepper

For me, the combination of spinach and blue cheese is a spectacular one. Any type of blue cheese is suitable for this wonderfully fresh-tasting salad, scattered with nutritious pumpkin seeds. Just use your favourite.

Put the spinach in a salad bowl and add the mushrooms, hard-boiled eggs and blue cheese. Mix together the garlic, fromage frais, mustard and lemon juice to make a dressing and toss carefully with the salad. Season to taste.

Arrange on serving plates, top with the avocado and toasted baguette slices and sprinkle over the toasted pumpkin seeds. Serve immediately.

P.G. TIPS

Other vegetables, such as leeks, artichokes and even asparagus, can be prepared in the same way for this salad. Pumpkin seeds are quite easy to find in health shops, but sunflower seeds make a tasty alternative if necessary.

Salad of Pickled Herrings, Jarlsberg, Potatoes & Dill

SERVES 4

500g (1lb 2oz) pickled herrings

400g (14oz) waxy potatoes

1 red onion, finely chopped

2 tablespoons white wine vinegar

6 (8) tablespoons olive oil

1 tablespoon crème fraîche

2 tablespoons chopped fresh dill

1 tablespoon sweet mustard

150g (5oz) Jarlsberg

Salt & freshly ground black pepper

ALTERNATIVE
CHEESES

Emmenthal, Cheddar, Havarti or Tilsit

Jarlsberg cheese is said by many to be a copy of the famous Swiss Emmenthal. I personally think it has a more delicate flavour and not such a nutty aftertaste. It is one of Norway's proudest treasures and deserves to be better known and more frequently used.

Cut the pickled herrings into large chunks and the Jarlsberg into batons. Cook the potatoes in boiling salted water until just tender, then drain. Leave until cool enough to handle, then peel and cut in half. Put them in a bowl and add the herrings and red onion.

Mix together the vinegar, oil, crème fraîche, dill and mustard to make a dressing. Pour the dressing over the potatoes, herrings and onions and toss lightly together, then season to taste. Transfer to a serving bowl, top with the batons of Jarlsberg and serve.

Roquefort & Red Cabbage Salad with Roasted Walnut Vinaigrette

SERVES 4

¼ red cabbage, central core removed, thinly sliced

4 (5) tablespoons red wine vinegar

50g (2oz, ⅓ cup) caster sugar

600ml (1 pint, 2½ cups) water

100g (4oz, ⅔ cup) streaky bacon, cut into 2cm (¾ in) dice

2 slices of white bread, cut into 1cm (½ in) cubes

1 garlic clove, crushed

2 heads of chicory

1 small head of radicchio

150g (5oz, generous ½ cup) Roquefort, crumbled

Salt & freshly ground black pepper

For the vinaigrette

4 (5) tablespoons red wine vinegar

1 teaspoon Dijon mustard

4 (5) tablespoons walnut oil

4 (5) tablespoons olive oil

2 tablespoons walnuts, roasted (see Tip) & broken into chunks

ALTERNATIVE
CHEESES

Any blue cheese

I am very fond of this salad. It always finds a place on my winter menus and is extremely pretty. The crunch of red cabbage and roasted walnuts makes an excellent combination with the sharp and tangy Roquefort. If Roquefort is not available, any blue cheese could be substituted, but I find the stronger ones such as Gorgonzola work best.

Put the cabbage in a bowl. Bring the vinegar to the boil, add the sugar and, once dissolved, pour it over the cabbage and stir well. Boil the water and pour that over the cabbage too. Leave to soak for 5 minutes, then drain in a colander and leave to cool.

Heat a frying pan over a high heat, add the bacon and cook until it is crisp and the fat has been released. Add the bread and fry until golden, then stir in the garlic and fry for 1 minute. Remove from the heat. Put the red cabbage in a salad bowl with the chicory and radicchio leaves, scatter over the bacon and croûtons and the Roquefort cheese.

Whisk together all the ingredients for the vinaigrette and pour it over the salad. Toss well, adjust the seasoning and serve.

P.G.TIPS

To roast nuts, toss them in a little oil, season lightly, then place on a baking sheet and bake in an oven preheated to 180°C, 350°F, gas 4 for 5–8 minutes, or until toasted in flavour and colour. Cool before use. I have on occasion replaced the red cabbage with finely shredded beetroot: a great alternative summer salad.

Cornish Crab & Asparagus Salad with Lemon, Mustard & Parmesan Vinaigrette

SERVES 4

12 asparagus spears, peeled & well trimmed

2 heads of chicory

2 avocados, peeled, stoned & sliced

2 carrots, cut into matchsticks

300g (11oz) fresh white crabmeat

Parmesan shavings, to garnish

Salt & freshly ground black pepper

For the lemon, mustard & Parmesan vinaigrette

1 tablespoon Dijon mustard

1 small egg yolk

1 tablespoon lemon juice

Finely grated zest of ¼ lemon

1 tablespoon champagne vinegar or white wine vinegar

5 (6) tablespoons extra-virgin olive oil

1½ tablespoons freshly grated Parmesan

Many years ago I worked in the West Country and discovered just how good the local ingredients could be. If you can get Cornish crab to use in this dish, for example, you will find it has an incomparable flavour. The salad makes a good first course for an early-summer meal.

Cook the asparagus spears in boiling salted water for 3–4 minutes or until just tender. Drain and refresh in cold water, then dry them thoroughly and cut lengthways in half.

For the dressing, whisk together the mustard, egg yolk, lemon juice and zest and vinegar, then whisk in the olive oil. Add the grated Parmesan cheese and season to taste.

Pull the leaves from the chicory, wash and dry them and arrange in a salad bowl or on serving plates. Put the asparagus, avocado, carrots and crabmeat in a separate bowl and toss gently with the dressing, then adjust the seasoning. Scatter this mixture over the chicory leaves, sprinkle some coarsely cracked black pepper over the top (see Tip on page 146) and then scatter with the Parmesan shavings. Serve immediately.

P.G.TIPS Vegetarians can easily omit the crabmeat and replace it with more vegetables. Globe artichoke hearts, for example, would go rather well.

Chilli-pickled Orange, Feta & Olive Salad

SERVES 4

4 oranges, preferably navel

90ml (3 fl oz, ⅓ cup) white wine vinegar

3 (4) tablespoons caster sugar

1 red chilli, thinly sliced into rings

90ml (3 fl oz, ⅓ cup) olive oil

2 tablespoons black olives, stoned

175g (6oz, ¾ cup) feta, cut into
1cm (½ in) cubes

1 tablespoon chopped fresh oregano
or parsley

Baby spinach and rocket leaves, to
garnish (optional)

Salt & freshly ground black pepper

ALTERNATIVE
CHEESES

Haloumi or a firm goat's cheese

In this tangy salad the oranges are marinated in vinegar and sugar overnight to give a refreshing sweet-and-sour flavour. Feta is a much-copied cheese and consequently the quality and flavour vary greatly, as does the type of milk used. Always try to obtain genuine Greek feta, which is generally made of 30 per cent goat's milk and 70 per cent sheep's milk.

Peel the oranges, being sure to remove all the white pith, and cut them into slices 5mm (¼ in) thick. Remove any pips and put the orange slices in a shallow dish. Boil the vinegar and sugar together for 2–3 minutes, add the chilli and then pour on to the orange slices. Cover and leave overnight.

The next day, drain off the juices from the pickled oranges into a bowl. Whisk in the olive oil to make a dressing and season with salt and pepper. Arrange the oranges in a serving bowl. Stir the olives, feta and oregano or parsley into the dressing and sprinkle it over the oranges. Sprinkle with coarsely cracked black pepper (see Tip on page 146), scatter over the spinach and rocket leaves, if using, and serve.

P.G. TIPS

Some people like to soak feta cheese in warm water or milk before using. This effectively softens the strong, salty flavour.

Radicchio, Mushroom & Chive Salad with Blue Cheese Yoghurt Dressing

SERVES 4

2 heads of radicchio
300g (11oz, 5 cups) button mushrooms, sliced
1 bunch of fresh chives
Salt & freshly ground black pepper

For the blue cheese yoghurt dressing
50g (2oz, ¼ cup) Stilton
1 tablespoon champagne vinegar
5 (6) tablespoons crème fraîche
3 (4) tablespoons Greek yoghurt
Juice of ½ lemon
Freshly grated nutmeg
1 tablespoon chopped fresh chives

ALTERNATIVE
CHEESES

Roquefort, dolcelatte or Cambazola

Radicchio is a bitter salad leaf that to my mind needs a contrasting partner. The blue cheese yoghurt dressing fits the bill perfectly. You could add some chopped hard-boiled egg, potatoes and French beans to make a more substantial dish for a main course.

First make the dressing. Put the Stilton in a bowl and mash well with a fork. Stir in the vinegar, then gently whisk in the crème fraîche and yoghurt. Squeeze in the lemon juice and season to taste with nutmeg, salt and pepper, then fold in the chives.

Separate the radicchio leaves, wash them and dry them well. Place in a bowl, add the sliced mushrooms and season lightly. Add the blue cheese dressing and toss carefully, then adjust the seasoning to taste. Arrange on serving plates, snip the chives into pieces 1cm (½ in) long and scatter over the top. Serve immediately.

P.G.TIPS

If you prefer a less tart dressing, add 1 tablespoon warmed honey, maple syrup or even good old sugar. Try adding a little grated orange rind to the dressing, too. Belgian endive or chicory has a similar bitter taste and could easily be substituted for the radicchio.

Insalata di Fontina

SERVES 4
....

225g (8oz) new potatoes

50g (2oz, ⅓ cup) prosciutto, cut into strips

100g (4oz, ½ cup) fontina, cut into batons

50g (2oz, ⅓ cup) mortadella, cut into batons

6 cocktail gherkins, cut lengthways into quarters

1 red onion, sliced into thin rings

225g (8oz) new potatoes

Salt & freshly ground black pepper

For the dressing
1 tablespoon chopped fresh oregano

¼ teaspoon Dijon mustard

2 canned anchovy fillets

2 tablespoons white wine vinegar

6 (8) tablespoons olive oil

ALTERNATIVE
....
CHEESES
....

Gruyère, Emmenthal, Port Salut or Tête de Moine

This hearty salad of cheese, ham and potatoes is substantial enough to serve as a main course. Salads that combine cheese and meat are very common in northern Europe. I devised this one with Italian flavourings in mind. The recipe has been in my repertoire since my early days as a chef and has remained one of my favourite salads. The original salad consists of shavings of Tête de Moine (monk's head), a cheese native to Switzerland. It is rather expensive and a little difficult to find except in specialist cheese shops, but well worth enquiring about. Fontina makes a more accessible and good substitute.

For the dressing, place the oregano and the mustard in a small bowl. Rinse the anchovy fillets to extract their salty flavour, then drain. Dry them well and chop finely. Add them to the bowl, pour over the vinegar and mix well together. Add the olive oil and whisk to form a light dressing. Season to taste and set aside.

Cook the potatoes in boiling salted water for about 20 minutes until just tender, then remove and cool slightly before peeling. Cut into 5mm (¼ in) thick slices and place in a bowl. While the potatoes are still warm, pour over the dressing and leave for 20 minutes to allow them to soak up the flavours.

Add the remaining ingredients and mix together. Pour on the dressing and toss again. Adjust the seasoning and serve.

Salad of Grilled Lamb Fillet with Lanark Blue & Warm Mint Dressing

SERVES 4

4 lamb fillets, about 75g (3oz) each

100g (4oz) French beans

8–12 thin slices cut from a ficelle loaf or small baguette

Olive oil, for brushing

A handful each of frisée & spinach leaves

2 tomatoes, skinned, deseeded & cut into strips

65g (2½ oz, generous 1 cup) button mushrooms, thinly sliced

50g (2oz, ¼ cup) Lanark Blue, diced

Salt & freshly ground black pepper

For the dressing

4 (5) tablespoons double cream

1 tablespoon clear honey

50g (2oz, ¼ cup) Lanark Blue, crumbled

1 tablespoon sherry vinegar

2 tablespoons olive oil

1 tablespoon chopped fresh mint

2 tablespoons hot water

ALTERNATIVE CHEESES

Stilton, Danish Blue, Bleu d'Auvergne or King Island (Aust)

Lamb and mint form a combination that everyone knows. I took it a stage further to create this wonderful salad. We are fortunate that we can still buy the Scottish cheese Lanark Blue. In 1995 its producer, Humphrey Errington, fought a 13-month battle in the courts to defend its reputation against health officials, who claimed that as a raw-milk cheese it could contain the bacterium Listeria and thus cause food poisoning. He finally won his case, and small cheesemakers throughout the UK owe him a huge debt for demonstrating that cheese made from unpasteurized milk carries no more risk to health than pasteurized cheese.

Season the lamb fillets and cook on a ridged cast-iron grill pan (or under a hot grill or in a frying pan) for 5–8 minutes, until done but still rosy inside. Keep warm.

Meanwhile, cook the French beans in boiling salted water until just tender, then drain and refresh in cold water. Drain again and dry.

For the dressing, put the cream and honey in a pan and bring to the boil, then remove from the heat. Add the cheese and allow it to melt into the cream. Whisk in the vinegar, olive oil and mint, then whisk in the water and season to taste.

Brush the slices of bread with olive oil and grill on both sides until they are lightly browned.

Put the frisée and spinach leaves in a bowl, add the tomatoes, French beans, mushrooms and cheese, then toss with the warm dressing. Put in the centre of 4 serving plates. Slice the grilled lamb fillets and arrange around the salad. Top the salad with the croûtons and serve immediately.

Chapter Four

Tagliatelle with Fried Egg, Capers & Pecorino Sardo

SERVES 4

500g (1lb 2oz) tagliatelle

Freshly grated nutmeg

40g (1½ oz, 3 tablespoons) unsalted butter

2 tablespoons superfine capers, rinsed & drained

4 free-range eggs

A little clarified butter (see Tip)

100g (4oz, 1 cup) pecorino Sardo, cut into shavings

Salt & freshly ground black pepper

A great and simple dish. When all that is needed is something quick but tasty, this fits the bill perfectly. Try adding crisply fried, diced pancetta to the pasta.

Cook the pasta in boiling salted water until *al dente*, then drain well and return to the pan. Season with nutmeg, salt and pepper, add the butter and capers and toss together well. Keep warm.

Quickly fry the eggs in clarified butter and season with salt. Arrange the pasta on warmed serving plates, top each portion with a fried egg and scatter over the pecorino shavings. Sprinkle with a little freshly cracked black pepper (see Tip on page 146) and serve.

P.G. TIPS

To clarify butter, heat gently in a small pan until it begins to boil. Boil for 2 minutes, then pour off the clarified butter through a fine conical strainer or a muslin-lined sieve, leaving the white, milky sediment in the pan. You should store clarified butter in the refrigerator.

Baked Bucatini with Garlic Cheese & Ricotta Sauce

SERVES 4
....

2 tablespoons extra-virgin olive oil

1 small garlic clove, crushed

150g (5oz, generous ½ cup) herb & garlic Boursin

125g (4½ oz, ½ cup) ricotta

150ml (¼ pint, ⅔ cup) crème fraîche

90ml (3 fl oz, ⅓ cup) single cream

2 tablespoons chopped fresh basil

450g (1lb) bucatini

Freshly grated nutmeg

75g (3oz, ¾ cup) Parmesan, freshly grated

Salt & freshly ground black pepper

ALTERNATIVE
....
CHEESE
....

Herb and garlic roulé

I have very strong views on cheeses with added flavourings and don't normally approve of them. In fact you will find only this and one other recipe (see page 168) using them in this book. But I am very fond of Boursin, partly because my parents liked it and it was always in our refrigerator at home.

Preheat the oven to 200°C, 400°F, gas 6. Heat half the olive oil in a pan, add the garlic and sweat until softened. Stir in the Boursin, ricotta, crème fraîche and single cream and cook for 1 minute. Stir in the chopped basil and season with salt and pepper.

Cook the bucatini in boiling salted water until *al dente*, then drain well. Return to the pan, stir in the remaining olive oil and season with nutmeg, salt and pepper. Transfer the pasta to a baking dish and pour over the cheese sauce. Sprinkle over the grated Parmesan and bake in the oven for about 10 minutes, until golden.

Stuffed Macaroni al Forno with Swiss Chard & Italian Cheeses

SERVES 4

500g (1lb 2oz) large macaroni, about 2cm (¾ in) in diameter

100g (4oz, ½ cup) dolcelatte, crumbled

25g (1oz, ¼ cup) Parmesan, freshly grated

Freshly grated nutmeg

Salt & freshly ground black pepper

For the stuffing

75g (3oz, 6 tablespoons) unsalted butter

1 onion, finely chopped

150g (5oz, scant 1 cup) Parma ham, chopped

500g (1lb 2oz) Swiss chard, roughly shredded

150g (5oz, generous ½ cup) ricotta

100g (4oz, 1 cup) Parmesan, freshly grated

1 egg yolk

For the sauce

50g (2oz, 4 tablespoons) unsalted butter

50g (2oz, ½ cup) plain flour

500ml (18 fl oz, 2¼ cups) milk, boiled & strained

ALTERNATIVE CHEESES

Any mild blue cheese is fine for this dish instead of the dolcelatte

Swiss chard was a very common vegetable in Britain in Victorian times and then fell into obscurity, but happily it is now regaining its popularity. It resembles spinach in flavour and is in season from September to March. Look out for red chard, with its striking beetroot-coloured leaves, as a change from the green variety.

Preheat the oven to 200°C, 400°F, gas 6. For the stuffing, heat the butter in a pan over a medium heat, add the onion and cook until lightly golden. Add the Parma ham and cook for 1 minute, then stir in the shredded chard and sweat for 3–4 minutes, until there is no moisture left in the pan. Transfer to a bowl and leave to cool. Meanwhile, cook the macaroni in plenty of boiling salted water until *al dente*, then drain and dry well.

Add the ricotta, Parmesan and egg yolk to the cooled Swiss chard mixture and stir together well. Season with nutmeg, salt and pepper. Put the mixture in a piping bag fitted with a plain nozzle and use to fill the macaroni. Put them in a well-buttered shallow ovenproof dish and set aside.

To make the sauce, melt the butter in a pan, add the flour and stir for 1–2 minutes to form a *roux*. Gradually stir in the milk until you have a smooth sauce, then leave to cook for 8–10 minutes over a very low heat. Season to taste with nutmeg, salt and pepper.

Pour the sauce over the stuffed macaroni, then sprinkle over the dolcelatte and Parmesan. Bake in the oven for 10–12 minutes or until a light golden crust forms. Allow to rest for 5 minutes before serving.

Topfenravioli with Prosciutto, Spinach & Foaming Brown Butter

SERVES 4

75g (3oz, 6 tablespoons) unsalted butter

450g (1lb) young spinach leaves

100g (4oz, ½ cup) cottage cheese,
well drained

75g (3oz, ½ cup) prosciutto, finely diced

50g (2oz, ¼ cup) buffalo or cow's milk
mozzarella, finely diced

2 tablespoons freshly grated Parmesan,
plus extra to serve

10 fresh basil leaves, roughly chopped,
plus a few whole leaves to garnish

Freshly grated nutmeg

Salt & freshly ground black pepper

For the pasta dough
250g (9oz, 2 cups) strong plain flour

A pinch of salt

1 tablespoon extra-virgin olive oil

2 eggs plus 1 egg yolk, lightly beaten

Crumbly cottage or curd cheese is used extensively in many German dishes. I particularly like the stuffing for this ravioli.

First make the pasta dough. Put the flour, salt and olive oil into a food processor and process for a few seconds to combine. Add the beaten eggs and process until the mixture forms a mass. This should only take a few seconds and it is important not to overwork the dough. Remove the dough from the food processor. It should be fairly soft and pliable. If it is too dry, knead in a little water; if it is too wet, sprinkle with a little flour. Cover with cling film and leave to rest at room temperature for 15–30 minutes.

Meanwhile, make the filling. Heat 25g (1oz, 2 tablespoons) of the butter in a large pan, add the spinach and cook for just a few minutes, until it has wilted and all the excess moisture has evaporated. Transfer to a bowl and leave to cool, then chop finely. Stir in the cottage cheese, prosciutto, mozzarella, Parmesan and chopped basil. Season to taste with nutmeg, salt and pepper.

Roll out the dough using a pasta machine if you have one. Alternatively, divide it into 2 batches and roll it out very thinly by hand. It should be so thin that it is almost translucent. Lightly brush 1 sheet of the dough with water, then put teaspoonfuls of stuffing on it about 5cm (2in) apart, in rows. Cover with the second sheet of pasta, press down gently, then cut round the stuffing with a round 6cm (2½ in) fluted pastry cutter. Check that the edges of the ravioli are well sealed.

Cook the ravioli in plenty of gently simmering salted water for 2–3 minutes, until *al dente*, then drain well. Heat the remaining butter in a frying pan until it is foaming, golden brown and smells nutty (the bottom of the pan will be covered with brown butter specks). Immediately drizzle the butter over the ravioli and sprinkle with more freshly grated Parmesan and a few basil leaves before serving.

TOPFENRAVIOLI WITH
PROSCIUTTO, SPINACH &
FOAMING BROWN BUTTER

Rigatoni with Mixed Peppers & Coriander & Goat's Cheese Pesto

SERVES 4

4 peppers (1 red, 1 green, 1 yellow, 1 orange)

50g (2oz, 4 tablespoons) unsalted butter

2 tablespoons olive oil

A pinch of sugar

450g (1lb) rigatoni

1 quantity of Coriander & Goat's Cheese Pesto (see page 20)

Salt & freshly ground black pepper

Fresh coriander leaves, to garnish (optional)

For an all-green version of this colourful pasta dish, you could substitute courgettes, leeks and broccoli for the peppers.

Halve and deseed the peppers, then cut them into strips 5mm (¼ in) wide. Heat the butter and oil in a frying pan, add the pepper strips and cook gently for 10–15 minutes. If they begin to stick to the pan, add a little water. When the peppers are tender, stir in the sugar and some salt and pepper to taste.

Cook the rigatoni in a large pan of boiling salted water until *al dente*, then drain well. Stir the pasta into the peppers, add the pesto sauce and lightly toss together. Adjust the seasoning, garnish with coriander leaves if liked, and serve straight away.

P.G.TIPS
For a really quick sauce, use bottled peppers in oil, and for a little variation why not try adding a few sautéed bacon lardons to the cooked pasta? Any other shaped pasta would look pretty in this dish.

Pennette al Dolcelatte

SERVES 4

450g (1lb) pennette

90ml (3 fl oz, ⅓ cup) double cream

100ml (3½ fl oz, ½ cup) Chicken Stock (see page 16) or Vegetable Stock (see page 16)

90g (3½ oz, scant ½ cup) dolcelatte, crumbled

4 (5) tablespoons extra-virgin olive oil

Freshly grated nutmeg

Salt & freshly ground black pepper

Freshly grated Parmesan, to serve (optional)

ALTERNATIVE
CHEESE

Try dolcelatte torta, which is a combination of mascarpone and dolcelatte, and omit the double cream

Although I have used pennette for this dish, any type of pasta may be substituted. To offset the richness of the sauce, I sometimes top the pasta with a light herb salad of basil, chives and oregano, mixed with a little frisée and dressed with balsamic vinaigrette.

Cook the pennette in plenty of boiling salted water until *al dente*. Meanwhile, bring the cream and stock to the boil, then remove from the heat and stir in the dolcelatte until smooth. Whisk in the olive oil to form a light sauce.

Drain the pasta and return it to the saucepan. Season with nutmeg, salt and pepper, then toss the pasta with the sauce. Serve immediately, with grated Parmesan if liked.

RIGATONI WITH
MIXED PEPPERS & CORIANDER
& GOAT'S CHEESE PESTO

Bel Paese Calzoni

SERVES 4

1 quantity of risen pizza dough
(see opposite)

Flour, for dusting

25g (1oz, ⅛ cup) ricotta

2 garlic cloves, crushed

2 tablespoons olive oil

75g (3oz, ⅓ cup) Bel Paese, rind removed,
coarsely chopped

100g (4oz, ⅔ cup) mortadella or
prosciutto, coarsely chopped

A little beaten egg

Vegetable oil for deep-frying (optional)

Salt & freshly ground black pepper

Calzone means pair of trousers! It is a sort of folded pizza, rather like a pasty, and is particularly delicious if you include lots of cheese so the molten cheese spills out when you cut into it. You can vary the fillings to your own taste – try mozzarella, salami or vegetables.

Knock back the risen dough, roll it out thinly on a floured surface and cut out eight 15cm (6in) rounds.

Mix together the ricotta, garlic, olive oil, Bel Paese and chopped mortadella or prosciutto and season to taste. Put the mixture on one half of each round of dough, leaving a border. Brush the edges of the dough with beaten egg and fold over to make turnovers. Crimp the edges for a neat finish.

Heat the vegetable oil in a large saucepan and fry the *calzoni* a few at a time for 5–6 minutes, until golden. Alternatively, brush them with a little beaten egg and bake in an oven preheated to 200°C, 400°F, gas 6 for about 12–15 minutes. Serve hot.

The Ultimate Vegetarian Calzoni

SERVES 4

1 quantity of risen pizza dough
(see opposite)

Flour, for dusting

6 (8) tablespoons olive oil

1 garlic clove, crushed

¼ teaspoon fennel seeds

1 aubergine, peeled & thinly sliced

1 fennel bulb, thinly sliced

150g (5oz, 1¼ cups) mozzarella, thinly
sliced

10 basil leaves, roughly chopped

A little beaten egg

Vegetable oil for deep-frying (optional)

Salt & freshly ground black pepper

To me, these calzoni *are lifted out of the ordinary by the inclusion of fennel, a much underrated vegetable which only the Italians seem to use to any great extent. Serve the* calzoni *with a tomato sauce, if you like.*

Knock back the risen dough, roll it out thinly on a floured surface and cut out eight 15cm (6in) rounds.

For the filling, heat the olive oil in a pan with the garlic and fennel seeds. Add the aubergine and fennel and cook gently for 12–15 minutes, until golden and tender. Add a little water to the vegetables if they begin to stick to the pan. Transfer to a bowl and leave to cool, then add the mozzarella and basil. Season to taste, then fill the turnovers, seal with a little beaten egg and cook as in the preceding recipe.

Roasted Vegetable Pizza with Goat's Cheese, Mozzarella & Rosemary Oil

SERVES 4

1 red pepper
90ml (3 fl oz, ⅓ cup) olive oil
1 courgette, thickly sliced
1 globe artichoke, cooked & cut into quarters
8 small, flat mushrooms, stalks removed
4 (5) tablespoons tomato passata
12 cherry tomatoes, cut in half
100g (4oz, ½ cup) goat's cheese, cut into 1cm (½ in) cubes
100g (4oz, ½ cup) mozzarella, cut into 1cm (½ in) cubes
Salt & freshly ground black pepper

For the dough
2 teaspoons dried yeast
300ml (½ pint, 1¼ cups) water
450g (1lb, 4 cups) strong plain flour
1 teaspoon salt
2 tablespoons olive oil

For the rosemary oil
1 garlic clove, crushed
2 tablespoons chopped fresh rosemary
90ml (3 fl oz, ⅓ cup) extra-virgin olive oil

A truly wonderful vegetarian pizza: roasted vegetables topped with contrasting cheeses and drizzled with rosemary oil. A real treat.

For the dough, dissolve the yeast in a little of the water. Sift the flour and salt into a bowl and make a well in the centre. Pour the yeast liquid into the well with the remaining water and the olive oil and bring it all together with your hands to form a pliable dough. Knead on a lightly floured surface for 6–8 minutes, until smooth and elastic. Place the dough in a lightly oiled bowl, cover with a damp cloth, then leave at warm room temperature for 1 hour or until doubled in size.

Meanwhile prepare the topping. Preheat the oven to 180°C, 350°F, gas 4. Brush the red pepper with a little of the olive oil, place in a baking dish and roast for 20 minutes. Add the remaining oil to the dish and put the courgette, artichoke and mushrooms in it. Season with salt and pepper and return to the oven for about 25 minutes or until all the vegetables are tender. Remove and leave to cool. Peel the skin off the pepper, cut it in half and remove the seeds. Cut the flesh into strips and set aside.

For the rosemary oil, blitz together the garlic and rosemary with the oil in a blender and set aside.

Raise the oven temperature to 200°C, 400°F, gas 6. Knock back the dough, divide it into 4 pieces and roll out each one into an 18cm (7in) circle (or if you're in a party mood, make one big pizza). Spread one quarter of the passata over each pizza base, then top with the roasted vegetables and the halved cherry tomatoes. Scatter both cheeses over the vegetables and drizzle over the rosemary oil. Bake for 15–20 minutes, until golden, then serve straight away.

Oyster & Spinach Pizza with Chorizo Sausage & Melting Dolcelatte

SERVES 4

6 (8) tablespoons olive oil

2 red onions, thinly sliced

450g (1lb) fresh spinach, washed

16 oysters, shucked (see Tip on page 30)

1 quantity of risen pizza dough
(see page 91)

250g (9oz, 1½ cups) chorizo sausage,
thinly sliced

175g (6oz, ¾ cup) dolcelatte, crumbled

Salt & freshly ground black pepper

ALTERNATIVE
CHEESES

Replace the dolcelatte with some shaved
pecorino or Gruyère

Dolcelatte and chorizo, a spicy Spanish sausage, make a delicious combination. Add the saltiness and soft texture of oysters and you have a creative and full-flavoured pizza.

Preheat the oven to 200°C, 400°F, gas 6. Heat one third of the oil in a pan, add the onions and fry for 10–12 minutes, until lightly golden. Season and remove from the pan. Heat half the remaining oil in the pan, add the spinach and cook for 2–3 minutes, until wilted. Season with salt and pepper and remove from the pan. Finally, add the rest of the oil to the pan and sauté the oysters for about 1 minute, just enough to seal them. Season and set aside.

Knock back the pizza dough and roll out into four 18cm (7in) rounds as in the preceding recipe. Distribute the spinach evenly over each pizza base. Arrange slices of chorizo on top, then dice the oysters and scatter them over. Scatter over the red onions and lastly the crumbled dolcelatte. Bake for 15 minutes or until the cheese is melted and bubbly. Serve straight away.

Suppli alla Gorgonzola con Basilico

SERVES 4

4 (5) tablespoons olive oil

1 onion, finely chopped

1 garlic clove, crushed

250g (9oz, 1⅓ cups) Arborio rice

500ml (18 fl oz, 2¼ cups) Chicken Stock (see page 16) or Cheese-infused Chicken Stock (see page 16)

50g (2oz, 4 tablespoons) unsalted butter

75g (3oz, ¾ cup) Parmesan, freshly grated

A good handful of fresh basil leaves

Freshly grated nutmeg

75g (3oz, scant ½ cup) Gorgonzola

3 (4) tablespoons plain flour

2 eggs, beaten

100g (4oz, 2 cups) fresh white breadcrumbs

Vegetable oil for deep-frying

Salt & freshly ground black pepper

These little rice fritters are a speciality of Campania, where they are made with mozzarella and known as suppli al telefono, *meaning telephone wires, because the molten cheese forms long strings when the fritters are cut open. My version is made with basil and creamy Gorgonzola, so you don't get the stringy effect of the cheese but you do get a wonderful, melting blue cheese fondue in the centre. Serve on a pool of tomato sauce.*

Heat half the olive oil in a heavy-based pan, add the onion and garlic and cook over a gentle heat until tender but not browned. Add the rice and stir well. Heat the stock to simmering point in a separate pan. Add a little of the stock to the rice and stir until it has been absorbed. Keep adding the stock, a ladleful at a time, stirring constantly, until the rice is tender but still firm to the bite. Stir in the butter and Parmesan, then spread the mixture out in a large baking tray and leave to cool.

Put the basil leaves in a blender (reserving a few to garnish the finished dish), add the remaining olive oil and blitz to a thickish purée. Stir the purée into the cooled rice, season to taste with nutmeg, salt and pepper and chill for at least 2 hours, preferably overnight.

To make the *suppli*, shape the rice mixture into 12–16 balls. Then cut the Gorgonzola into 12–16 pieces and push a piece into the centre of each rice ball. Re-form them neatly, pulling the rice back over the cheese and making sure it is completely enclosed. Coat the rice balls in the flour, then in the beaten egg and finally in the breadcrumbs.

Heat the vegetable oil in a deep-fat fryer or a deep saucepan and fry the *suppli* in batches for 2–3 minutes, until golden. Drain well on kitchen paper and then serve immediately, garnished with the reserved basil.

P.G.TIPS

Suppli can also be made with plain boiled rice and can be stuffed with a variety of fillings, one of my favourites being a mixture of sautéed chicken livers, prosciutto and wild mushrooms. For a vegetarian option, try sun-dried tomatoes and sautéed aubergine, and, of course, use vegetable stock instead.

Asparagus Risotto with Fonduta

SERVES 4

16 asparagus spears, peeled & well trimmed

125g (4½ oz, 9 tablespoons) unsalted butter

2 shallots, finely diced

250g (9oz, 1⅓ cups) Arborio rice

600ml (1 pint, 2½ cups) Cheese-infused Chicken Stock (see page 17)

90ml (3 fl oz, ⅓ cup) dry white wine

Salt & freshly ground black pepper

For the fonduta

190g (6½ oz, ⅔ cup) fontina, rind removed, thinly sliced

5 (6) tablespoons milk

15g (½ oz, 1 tablespoon) unsalted butter

2 egg yolks

1½ tablespoons double cream

ALTERNATIVE
CHEESES

Beaufort, Jarlsberg, Gruyère or Emmenthal

Fonduta is one of Italy's great classic sauces and I use it a lot with pasta and vegetables. Here it makes a creamy addition to an asparagus risotto. Lightly sautéed wild mushrooms can be stirred into the risotto with the asparagus for added flavour, if liked.

For the *fonduta*, put the cheese in a pan with the milk and leave for 2 hours.

Meanwhile, cook the asparagus in boiling salted water for 5 minutes or until just tender. Drain, refresh in cold water and then dry. Cut into thin diagonal slices and set aside.

Put the butter for the *fonduta* in a stainless steel or glass bowl set over a pan of gently simmering water, making sure the water does not touch the base of the bowl. When it has melted, add the milk-soaked cheese. Stir until the cheese has melted and the mixture has become more solid. Stir in the egg yolks, one at a time. At this stage the mixture will become runny again. Stir constantly until the sauce has thickened, making sure it does not become too hot or it will curdle. Add the cream and keep warm.

For the risotto, melt 100g (4oz, 8 tablespoons) of the butter in a saucepan, add the shallots and cook gently until softened but not browned. Add the rice and stir until coated with the butter. Heat the stock to simmering point in a separate pan. Add the white wine and a little of the stock to the rice and stir until the liquid has been absorbed. Keep adding the stock, a ladleful at a time, stirring constantly, until the rice is tender but still retains a bite. Towards the end of cooking, add the stock in smaller quantities and check if the rice is done. It should take about 25 minutes in all.

Add enough of the *fonduta* to the risotto to give a loose but not sloppy consistency. Melt the remaining butter in a pan and quickly reheat the asparagus in it. Stir the asparagus into the risotto, adjust the seasoning and divide between 4 serving plates. Serve immediately.

P.G.TIPS

I like asparagus to be well trimmed before cooking. Snap off the white woody part from the base of each spear, then peel away the skin from the base to the bud at the tip. The older and coarser the asparagus, the more trimming it will need.

Crispy Cheese Risotto al Salto

SERVES 4

250g (9oz, about 2 cups) leftover risotto

25g (1oz, ¼ cup) Parmesan, freshly grated

50g (2oz, ½ cup) fontina or Emmenthal, grated

3 (4) tablespoons vegetable oil

15g (½ oz, 1 tablespoon) unsalted butter, melted

Salt & freshly ground black pepper

This is a very good way of using up leftover risotto and in fact it is worth making extra just for this. A crispy fried risotto cake, it makes an ideal accompaniment to a classic osso buco in a rich tomato sauce, or you can serve it with grilled vegetables for a vegetarian dish.

Mix the cooked risotto with both cheeses and season well with salt and pepper. Heat a heavy-based frying pan over a high heat. Add the oil and then the rice and cheese mixture, packing it down well to form a cake about 1–2cm (½–¾ in) thick. Reduce the heat and cook for about 5 minutes, until golden and crisp around the edges. Turn the cake over and cook for a further 5 minutes, until golden and crispy. Turn out on to a serving dish, brush with the melted butter and serve cut into wedges.

Baked Walnut Gnocchi with Asiago & Gruyère

SERVES 4

350g (12oz) potatoes (preferably King Edward or Maris Piper), peeled & cut into chunks

75g (3oz, ¾ cup) walnuts, ground

75g (3oz, ¾ cup) Asiago, grated

15g (½ oz, 1 tablespoon) unsalted butter

2 egg yolks

125g (4½ oz, generous 1 cup) plain flour

Freshly grated nutmeg

Salt & freshly ground black pepper

For the topping

50g (2oz, 4 tablespoons) unsalted butter

1 tablespoon roughly chopped fresh flat-leaf parsley

50g (2oz, ½ cup) Gruyère, finely grated

25g (1oz, ¼ cup) Asiago, finely grated

Walnuts and nutty-flavoured Gruyère are a great combination and this makes an excellent dish for autumn. For a real treat, sauté some fresh ceps with garlic and parsley, then put them on top of the poached gnocchi before adding the two cheeses.

Cook the potatoes in boiling salted water until tender, then drain well. Mash them while they are still hot. Add the walnuts and Asiago and beat well to allow the cheese to melt. Mix in the butter, egg yolks and half the flour, then season with nutmeg, salt and pepper. Turn the mixture out on to a lightly floured work surface and knead in the remaining flour, a little at a time, to form a smooth, soft but not sloppy dough. Leave to cool.

Roll out the dough into long cylinders 2.5cm (1in) thick and cut them into 2cm (¾ in) lengths. Roll each piece over the prongs of a fork to form the classic ridged and slightly curved gnocchi shape. Place the gnocchi on a floured baking tray and leave them to dry for about 1 hour.

Preheat the oven to 180°C, 350°F, gas 4. Poach the gnocchi a few at a time in a large pan of boiling salted water until they rise to the surface, about 2–3 minutes. Remove with a slotted spoon and arrange in a lightly greased, shallow, ovenproof dish.

For the sauce, melt the butter and pour it over the gnocchi, then sprinkle them with the parsley, Gruyère and Asiago. Bake for 12–15 minutes or until the top is brown and crisp. Serve while still bubbling.

Malfattini of Ricotta & Rocket with Pecorino & White Truffle Oil Sauce

SERVES 4

25g (1oz, 2 tablespoons) unsalted butter

175g (6oz) rocket, plus a few leaves to garnish

400g (14oz, 1¾ cups) ricotta, sieved

150g (5oz, 1¼ cups) plain flour

2 eggs

1 egg yolk

100g (4oz, 1 cup) Parmesan, freshly grated, plus extra to serve

Freshly grated nutmeg

Salt & freshly ground black pepper

For the sauce

150g (5oz, 1¼ cups) pecorino Sardo, coarsely grated

50g (2oz, 4 tablespoons) unsalted butter

50g (2oz, ¼ cup) mascarpone

150ml (¼ pint, ⅔ cup) milk

2 tablespoons white truffle oil

The original recipe for these little gnocchi calls for sliced fresh Piedmont truffles – delicious but so expensive! Replace them with white truffle oil which is reasonably priced in comparison and available from specialist delicatessens. If you do happen to get hold of a white truffle, grate it over the top. Malfattini means misshapen, which is appropriate as these are not the usual gnocchi shape. The sauce is a variation of the classic fonduta *(see page 96) but uses pecorino instead of fontina.*

Heat the butter in a pan, add the rocket and cook for 1 minute, until wilted. Leave to cool and then chop finely.

Put the ricotta, flour, eggs and egg yolk in a bowl and mix well together. Stir in the Parmesan and rocket and season with nutmeg, salt and pepper. Shape the mixture into ovals with 2 wet dessertspoons, turning it between them. Drop them in batches into a large pan of lightly simmering salted water and cook until they rise to the surface. Remove with a slotted spoon and drain on kitchen paper. Keep them warm while you make the sauce.

Put the pecorino, butter, mascarpone and milk in a bowl set over a pan of simmering water, making sure the water isn't touching the base of the bowl. Let the cheese melt slowly, whisking occasionally, then whisk in the truffle oil until the mixture comes together into a sauce. Season to taste.

To serve, warm the *malfattini* through in a low oven for a couple of minutes if necessary, then arrange them in serving bowls. Pour over the sauce, garnish with rocket and sprinkle with a little extra Parmesan.

Chapter Five

Red Mullet on Baked Salad Caprese with Basil & Olive Oil

SERVES 4

2 balls of cow's milk mozzarella, cut into slices 1cm (½ in) thick

8 plum tomatoes, skinned & cut into slices 1cm (½ in) thick

4 × 175g (6oz) red mullet fillets, skin on

A small bunch of fresh basil

150ml (¼ pint, ⅔ cup) extra-virgin olive oil

Salt & freshly ground black pepper

A simple dish with fresh summer flavours. Caprese is the name given to the famous Italian salad of mozzarella, tomato and basil. Here the tomato and cheese serve as a bed for red mullet, which is scattered liberally with fresh basil leaves. (See the photograph on page 2.)

Preheat the oven to 220°C, 425°F, gas 7. Lightly oil a shallow ovenproof dish large enough to hold the red mullet fillets in a single layer. Then arrange overlapping alternate slices of mozzarella and tomato over the base of the dish and season with salt and pepper. Lay the mullet fillets on top, skin-side up, season, then scatter over the basil leaves and pour over the olive oil. Bake for 8–10 minutes and then serve immediately.

P.G.TIPS
I like to serve this dish with some buttery noodles. Sometimes I vary it by adding some diced black olives to the pasta, or even a few sun-dried tomatoes.

Parmesan-crusted Sea Bass with Thyme-grilled Vegetables

SERVES 4

75g (3oz, ¾ cup) Parmesan, freshly grated

25g (1oz, ½ cup) fresh white breadcrumbs

Zest of ½ lemon

4×175g (6oz) sea bass fillets, skin on

2 eggs, beaten

4 (5) tablespoons vegetable oil

25g (1oz, 2 tablespoons) unsalted butter

Salt & freshly ground black pepper

For the vegetables

250g (9oz, 2 cups) courgettes, cut into slices 5mm (¼ in) thick

12 asparagus spears, peeled & well trimmed

2 cooked globe artichoke hearts, cut into quarters

1 tablespoon fresh thyme leaves

4 (5) tablespoons olive oil

2 tablespoons aged balsamic vinegar

Any firm fish would be suitable for this dish. You need to grill the vegetables with the thyme a day in advance and leave them overnight so that their juices run. The juices are then mixed with balsamic vinegar, making a delicious, thyme-scented vinaigrette to drizzle over the fish.

Put the courgettes, asparagus and cooked artichokes on a baking tray, season, then sprinkle over the thyme leaves and toss with the olive oil. Grill over a barbecue (or under a preheated grill) for about 5–6 minutes, until the vegetables are slightly charred all over but still retain a bite. Leave overnight in the refrigerator, covered with cling film.

The next day, drain the juices from the vegetables and reserve. Preheat the oven to 180°C, 350°F, gas 4.

Mix together the Parmesan, breadcrumbs, lemon zest and some seasoning. Season the bass fillets on both sides with salt and pepper. Put the beaten eggs in a shallow dish and dip the fish in them to coat both sides, then dip the fish in the Parmesan mixture, pressing it on well.

Reheat the grilled vegetables in the oven. Whisk 3 (4) tablespoons of the reserved cooking juices with the balsamic vinegar.

Heat the oil and butter in a large frying pan until foaming, then add the Parmesan-coated fish fillets. Cook for about 3–4 minutes per side, until golden and crisp. To serve, arrange the thyme-grilled vegetables on serving plates, top with the bass and drizzle around the vinaigrette.

P.G.TIPS

For variation, rosemary and oregano could replace the thyme, while other good grilling vegetables such as peppers and aubergines could be substituted for the courgettes, asparagus and artichokes. Aged balsamic vinegar is best.

Saffron-grilled Cod Fillet with Aligot & Beurre d'Escargot

SERVES 4

4 (5) tablespoons olive oil

1 tablespoon lemon juice

¼ teaspoon saffron strands

4×150g (5oz) cod fillets, skin on

1 quantity of freshly prepared Aligot (see page 135)

Salt & freshly ground black pepper

For the beurre d'escargot

150g (5oz, 10 tablespoons) unsalted butter

2 garlic cloves, crushed

3 (4) tablespoons chopped fresh flat-leaf parsley, plus a few sprigs to garnish

¼ teaspoon Dijon mustard

2 tablespoons lemon juice

Beurre d'escargot *tastes so good that it seems a shame to reserve it for serving with snails. Here it is poured over grilled cod, served on a meltingly rich potato and cheese purée. The smell when it hits the table is something else! I like to accompany this dish with some French beans or grilled leeks.*

Put the olive oil, lemon juice and saffron in a pan and warm through to infuse the flavours. Pour this over the cod fillets and leave to marinate, either for 2 hours at room temperature or overnight in the refrigerator.

Next prepare the butter, which can be done well ahead of time. Melt the butter over a low heat, then add the garlic. Raise the heat a little and lightly fry the garlic without letting it colour. Stir in the chopped parsley and mustard, then pour into a bowl and leave to cool. Add the lemon juice and season to taste.

To cook the cod, remove it from the marinade, season well and place on a ridged cast-iron grill pan or under a preheated grill. Cook until tender and golden, about 3–4 minutes per side on a grill pan or 5–6 minutes per side under a grill. (You could also fry the fish.)

To serve, put a good dollop of aligot on each serving plate and top with the cod. Reheat the parsley and garlic butter and pour it over the fish, then garnish with sprigs of parsley.

P.G.TIPS Another way to serve the fish is to cook it lightly as usual, then to top it with a light mixture of fresh breadcrumbs, mustard and butter and brown it under a hot grill before setting it down on the aligot.

Wing of Skate with Camembert, Spinach, Lardons & Cider

SERVES 4

75g (3oz, ½ cup) streaky bacon in a piece, cut into 5mm (¼in) dice

150g (5oz, 2½ cups) button mushrooms, cut into 5mm (¼in) dice

4 (5) tablespoons crème fraîche

450g (1lb) spinach, washed

½ small Camembert, cut into 5mm (¼in) dice

4 × 300g (11oz) skate wings

4 pieces of *crépinette*, about 25cm (10in) square

5 (6) tablespoons dry cider

150ml (¼ pint, ⅔ cup) dry white wine

150ml (¼ pint, ⅔ cup) Chicken Stock (see page 16)

40g (1½ oz, 3 tablespoons) unsalted butter, chilled & diced, plus a little melted butter for brushing

2 tablespoons olive oil

1 tablespoon grainy mustard

Salt & freshly ground black pepper

ALTERNATIVE
CHEESE

Cooleeney, sometimes known as Irish Camembert

This dish calls for the skate to be enclosed in crépinette *(pig's caul), which seals in the filling and keeps the fish moist. A good butcher should be able to get it for you. You will need 4 very thin pieces.*

Preheat the oven to 200°C, 400°F, gas 6. Heat a frying pan until smoking, add the bacon lardons and fry over a high heat until crisp. Add the mushrooms and fry for 2 minutes. Stir in the crème fraîche and cook until reduced by half. Then stir in the spinach, remove from the heat and leave to cool. Add the diced Camembert and some seasoning.

Coat each skate wing with the Camembert and spinach mixture, spreading it evenly with a palette knife. Brush the pieces of *crépinette* with melted butter, then put the skate on them, stuffing-side down. Wrap the fish well in the *crépinette* and put it in an ovenproof dish large enough to hold it in a single layer. Pour the cider, wine and chicken stock around the skate and bake for 12–15 minutes, until tender. Remove the fish and keep warm. Strain the juices into a clean pan and whisk in the butter and olive oil a little at a time to form a sauce. Stir in the mustard and adjust the seasoning. Arrange the skate wings on a serving dish, pour over the sauce and serve.

P.G.TIPS

Other white-fleshed fish such as brill or turbot could replace the skate. Swiss chard or even finely shredded cabbage are good alternatives to the spinach.

Wine-roasted Turbot on the Bone with Wilted Chicory & Bleu d'Auvergne

SERVES 4

50g (2oz, 4 tablespoons) softened unsalted butter

75g (3oz, scant ½ cup) Bleu d'Auvergne

2 tablespoons chopped fresh coriander

4 (5) tablespoons vegetable oil

4×200g (7oz) turbot steaks on the bone

150ml (¼ pint, ⅔ cup) dry white wine

150ml (¼ pint, ⅔ cup) Reduced Meat Stock (see page 17)

Salt & freshly ground black pepper

For the chicory
2 heads of chicory

25g (1oz, 2 tablespoons) unsalted butter

½ teaspoon sugar

For the salad
1 tablespoon walnut oil

2 tablespoons olive oil

1 tablespoon champagne vinegar

250g (9oz) lamb's lettuce (mâche)

ALTERNATIVE
CHEESES

Cashel Blue or Bleu des Causses

Fish and blue cheese are a rare combination but I find they work surprisingly well here. Cooking fish on the bone is a useful technique which helps keep it moist and succulent.

Preheat the oven to 190°C, 375°F, gas 5. Beat the butter, Bleu d'Auvergne and coriander together and set aside.

Heat the oil in an ovenproof frying pan or a shallow flameproof casserole large enough to hold the fish in one layer. Season the turbot and fry in the oil for about 2 minutes on each side, until golden. Pour on the wine and stock and place in the oven for 10 minutes or until the fish is cooked through, basting it with the juices once or twice.

Meanwhile, remove the leaves from the chicory, wash them and cut them lengthways into narrow strips. Put them in a pan with the butter and sugar and cook for 8–10 minutes, until all the liquid has evaporated and the chicory is tender and lightly caramelized. Season to taste and keep warm.

For the salad, whisk together the oils and vinegar and season to taste, then toss with the lamb's lettuce.

Remove the fish from the oven, strain the juices into a pan and keep warm over a low heat. Keep the fish warm. Heat the cheese and coriander butter in a frying pan until it is foaming and smells nutty. Add the foaming butter to the juices from the fish and season to taste. Arrange the chicory on warm serving plates, top with the roasted turbot and pour the sauce around. Serve immediately, accompanied by the salad.

P.G.TIPS

Chicory is most often found in salads nowadays but it has a wonderful flavour if cooked gently in butter with a little sugar to offset the bitterness. Experiment by flavouring it with spices and/or orange juice as well.

Stuffed Sardines with Parmesan Gremolata & Caper Butter

Sardines have become newly fashionable over the past few years, and, what's more, they're good for us and very reasonably priced. This Parmesan, fennel and lemon stuffing goes nicely with them. Mackerel can be used instead of sardines, if you prefer.

SERVES 4

24 fresh sardines, about 15cm (6in) long, scaled

4 (5) tablespoons olive oil

2 garlic cloves, crushed

1 fennel bulb, with its green feathery leaves, finely chopped

1 tablespoon chopped fresh thyme

1 tablespoon chopped fresh oregano

Zest of 1 lemon

1 tablespoon Pernod or other aniseed liqueur

25g (1oz, ½ cup) fresh white breadcrumbs

50g (2oz, ½ cup) Parmesan, freshly grated

Freshly grated nutmeg

Salt & freshly ground black pepper

For the caper butter

125g (4½ oz, 5 tablespoons) unsalted butter

2 shallots, finely chopped

3 (4) tablespoons superfine capers, rinsed & drained

1 tablespoon chopped fresh parsley

Juice of 1 lemon

ALTERNATIVE
CHEESES

Grana padana (a cheaper version of Parmesan), Asiago or pecorino

Preheat the oven to 200°C, 400°F, gas 6. Slit the sardines open along the belly and carefully pull out the entrails. Open the fish flat and carefully pull out the backbone from the head to the tail, snipping it off at the tail end with scissors and leaving the head and tail intact. Set the fish aside.

Heat half the oil in a pan, add the garlic and cook gently until tender. Add the fennel and cook for 5 minutes. Then stir in the herbs, lemon zest and Pernod, followed by the breadcrumbs and Parmesan. Season to taste with nutmeg, salt and pepper and remove from the heat.

Fill the cavity of each sardine with this mixture, pressing it in well. Put the fish on an oiled baking sheet, brush them with the remaining oil and bake for 8–10 minutes, until cooked through.

For the caper butter, melt the butter over a low heat, then add the shallots, capers and parsley. Cook until the butter begins to foam and becomes nutty in fragrance. Add the lemon juice, then immediately pour the butter over the sardines and serve.

Gratin of Lobster with Parmesan & Tarragon Sauce

SERVES 4

4 cooked lobsters, weighing about 500g (1lb 2oz) each

25g (1oz, 2 tablespoons) unsalted butter

Cayenne pepper, to taste

5 (6) tablespoons dry white wine

1 tablespoon chopped fresh tarragon, plus a few sprigs to garnish

300ml (½ pint, 1¼ cups) Basic Cheese Sauce (see page 18)

4 (5) tablespoons double cream, semi-whipped

3 (4) tablespoons freshly grated Parmesan

Salt & freshly ground black pepper

This is based on that great dish, lobster Thermidor. All you need to serve with it is a simple rice pilaff.

Cut the claws off the lobster with a large knife, then split the lobster in half down the back: the easiest way to do this is to put a large knife through the centre of the body section and cut down through the head, then take out the knife, turn the lobster round and cut down the centre of the body through the tail. Remove and discard the head sac and the intestinal vein, then take out the lobster meat from the head and tail and cut it into large cubes. Discard the gills (known as 'dead men's fingers') from the lobster shells and reserve the shells. Crack the claws in 2 or 3 places and pick out the meat.

Heat the butter in a pan, add the lobster meat and season with salt, pepper and cayenne. Pour in the white wine, bring to the boil and simmer for 1 minute – no longer or the lobster will toughen. Remove the lobster from the pan with a slotted spoon and continue to boil the wine until it is reduced by half its volume. Stir in the chopped tarragon and the cheese sauce, then fold in the cream and return the lobster to the pan. Adjust the seasoning.

Fill the 8 lobster shells with the sauce, put them on a baking sheet or in a shallow gratin dish and sprinkle with the grated Parmesan. Brown under a hot grill and then serve, garnished with sprigs of tarragon.

Sizzling Prawns with Sofrito, Peppers & Manchego

SERVES 4

4 (5) tablespoons olive oil

50g (2oz, 4 tablespoons) unsalted butter

2 garlic cloves, crushed

20–24 large raw prawns, shelled & deveined

1 red onion, cut into wedges about 5mm (¼ in) thick

2 red peppers, halved, deseeded & cut into strips 1cm (½ in) wide

1 green pepper, halved, deseeded & cut into strips 1cm (½ in) wide

300g (11oz, 2 cups) tomatoes, skinned, deseeded & chopped

A pinch of cayenne pepper

½ teaspoon paprika

250g (9oz, generous 1 cup) Manchego, cut into 2cm (¾ in) cubes

2 tablespoons fresh coriander leaves

Salt & freshly ground black pepper

ALTERNATIVE
CHEESE

Feta

Manchego is Spain's best-known cheese and, when fresh, has a mild, creamy consistency. Many Spanish recipes begin with instructions to prepare a sofrito – onions, garlic, tomatoes and sometimes parsley, cooked slowly to make a thick, intensely flavoured savoury base. This particular dish is of Mexican-Spanish origin and could be made with almost any seafood. Try lobster or scallops for an extravagant version. Saffron rice makes a good accompaniment.

Heat the oil and butter in a frying pan until the butter is foaming, then add the garlic and cook for 1 minute. Throw in the prawns and sauté them over a fairly high heat for about 1–2 minutes, until coloured. Remove from the pan and keep warm. Add the onion and peppers to the pan, cover and cook over a low heat for 15 minutes, until softened.

Stir in the tomatoes, cayenne and paprika and cook for about 5 minutes, until the tomatoes begin to break down. Return the prawns to the pan, stir together, then add the Manchego and sauté for 30 seconds. Season to taste, scatter over the fresh coriander and serve immediately.

SIZZLING PRAWNS
WITH SOFRITO, PEPPERS
& MANCHEGO

Mussel Fondue Normandie

SERVES 6 as a starter,
4 as a main course

225g (8oz, 1 cup) Emmenthal, grated

1 tablespoon cornflour

½ garlic clove

300ml (½ pint, 1¼ cups) dry white wine

250g (9oz, generous 1 cup) very ripe
Camembert, rind removed, cut into
small pieces

6 (8) tablespoons dry cider

Freshly grated nutmeg

Salt & freshly ground black pepper

For the mussels

900g (2lb) mussels

1 shallot, finely chopped

A few parsley stalks

175ml (6 fl oz, ¾ cup) dry white wine

I think that it's fair to say that most cheese dishes simply include a little cheese rather than use it as the main ingredient. One exception is fondue, a dish invented in the Swiss Alps to use the famous cheeses of the region, Emmenthal and Gruyère. My favourite fondue combines Emmenthal with Camembert from Normandy for a tasty modern variation. It is very important to have a proper fondue pot. This is easy to find and well worth a small investment in order to keep your fondue at the right temperature.

First clean the mussels. Scrub them under cold running water, pulling out their 'beards' and scraping off any barnacles with a knife. Discard any open mussels that do not close when tapped lightly on a work surface.

For the fondue, gently toss the Emmenthal with the cornflour and set aside. Rub the inside of a fondue pot or earthenware casserole with the cut surface of the garlic. Pour in the white wine and cook over a low heat until it just starts to bubble. Gradually stir in the Emmenthal and keep stirring until smooth. Then add the Camembert and blend together until the Camembert melts and the mixture is smooth again. Add the cider, season with salt, pepper and nutmeg, and keep warm.

Place the mussels in a pan with the shallot, parsley stalks and white wine, cover with a tight-fitting lid and place over a high heat, shaking the pan once or twice, until the mussels have opened (about 3–4 minutes). Drain them in a colander, reserving the cooking liquid, and discard any mussels that remain closed. Remove the mussels from their shells and keep warm. Strain the cooking liquid and add to the fondue. Serve the mussels with fondue forks to dip into the Camembert fondue.

P.G.TIPS
Any seafood would be good instead of mussels. I sometimes serve the fondue with new potatoes: dip them into the pot too – delicious!

Chicken Schnitzel with Mozzarella, Tomato Tapenade & Basil

SERVES 4

4 × 150g (5oz) skinless boneless chicken breasts

Flour, for dusting

1 egg, beaten

4 (5) tablespoons fresh white breadcrumbs

4 (5) tablespoons olive oil

100g (4oz, ½ cup) unsalted butter

1 ball of mozzarella, cut into 8 slices

2 tablespoons roughly chopped fresh basil

Juice of ½ lemon

Salt & freshly ground black pepper

For the tomato tapenade

75g (3oz, 1½ cups) sun-dried tomatoes

25g (1oz) superfine capers, rinsed & drained

2 garlic cloves, crushed

4 (5) tablespoons oil from the sun-dried tomatoes

The classic combination of mozzarella, tomato and basil in a different guise. You can use turbot or a similar white fish instead of chicken and it works just as well. Tomato tapenade is now available in jars in many supermarkets but I still think that home-made is better. Besides, it's really quick to make your own. You won't need to use all of it in this recipe but it keeps well in the refrigerator.

For the tapenade, put all the ingredients in a blender and blitz to a coarse purée (do not purée it too finely or it will become mushy).

Put the chicken breasts between 2 sheets of cling film and beat lightly with a meat mallet or the end of a rolling pin until they are just under 5mm (¼in) thick. Season with salt and pepper, then dust lightly with flour. Dip them in the beaten egg and then in the breadcrumbs. Brush off any excess crumbs.

Heat the olive oil and 25g (1oz, 2 tablespoons) of the butter in a frying pan and add the chicken. Cook for about 4–5 minutes on each side, until the chicken is golden and cooked through, then transfer to heatproof serving plates. Top each chicken breast with 2 slices of mozzarella, then spread ½ tablespoon of tomato tapenade over the cheese. Place under a hot grill until the mozzarella begins to soften.

Meanwhile, heat the remaining butter in a frying pan until it is foaming and smells nutty. Add the basil and lemon juice, pour it over the chicken and serve immediately.

P.G. TIPS

Sometimes I make this with tomato tapenade spread over one slice of mozzarella and black olive tapenade on the other. The contrast of black, red and white looks spectacular. (Olive tapenade is available in jars in most supermarkets.)

Grilled Chicken Spatchcock with Tomme, Ricotta Verde & Sweet Shallot Vinaigrette

SERVES 4

4×400g (14oz) poussins, free-range if possible

75g (3oz, scant ½ cup) white Tomme

75g (3oz, scant ½ cup) ricotta

1 bunch of watercress, stalks removed, leaves finely chopped

2 tablespoons chopped fresh basil

1 shallot, finely chopped

1 garlic clove, crushed

2 tablespoons olive oil

Lemon wedges, to serve

Salt & freshly ground black pepper

For the marinade

1 garlic clove, crushed

Juice & zest of 2 lemons

4 (5) tablespoons olive oil

For the vinaigrette

4 shallots, finely sliced

10g (¼oz, ½ tablespoon) unsalted butter

A pinch of sugar

1 tablespoon champagne vinegar

4 (5) tablespoons olive oil

¼ teaspoon Dijon mustard

I recently discovered spatchcocked poussins in a major supermarket. What a superb idea! All the work has been done for you. If you are not lucky enough to find them, don't be too alarmed at the thought of preparing the birds yourself. After a few attempts you'll wonder what all the fuss was about. Your guests will be impressed too. Serve the chickens with a watercress salad and new potatoes.

To spatchcock the poussins, you simply need to open them out flat. To do this, cut out the backbone with kitchen scissors or poultry shears. Break the wishbone, then turn each bird cut-side down and flatten it by pressing down with the heel of your hand. Turn it over and remove all the ribcage bones.

Mix together all the ingredients for the marinade, season with salt and pepper and pour into a large shallow container – you might need 2 to hold the poussins. Add the poussins, turning them to coat, cover and leave to marinate for at least 4 hours, but preferably overnight, in the refrigerator.

To make the vinaigrette, gently fry the shallots in the butter with the sugar until golden and lightly caramelized. Whisk together the vinegar, oil, mustard and some salt and pepper. Add the hot shallots and leave to cool. (This can be done several hours in advance.)

In a bowl, mix together the Tomme, ricotta, watercress, basil, shallot, garlic and olive oil. Season to taste. Remove the poussins from the marinade and dry well. Carefully loosen the skin of each bird without detaching it and push the stuffing underneath, spreading it over the flesh – it's easiest to use your fingers. Smooth the skin over again and season with salt and pepper.

Grill the poussins for about 7–8 minutes on each side, until tender and cooked through. A charcoal grill would be ideal but you could use a ridged grill pan instead, or fry them. Put them on warmed serving plates, drizzle over a little of the vinaigrette and serve the rest on the side. Accompany with lemon wedges.

P.G.TIPS
If you find it difficult removing the ribcage from the raw poussins, take out the bones after the birds have been cooked. They will come away much more easily.

Quails Stuffed with Sage Derby & Muscat Grapes

SERVES 4

8 quails, boned (ask your butcher to do this & give you the bones, if possible)

100g (4oz, ½ cup) softened unsalted butter

100g (4oz, 1 cup) Sage Derby, grated

1 shallot, finely chopped

1 small garlic clove, crushed

Salt & freshly ground black pepper

For the sauce

90ml (3 fl oz, ⅓ cup) white wine

300ml (½ pint, 1¼ cups) Reduced Meat Stock (see page 17)

350g (12oz) muscat grapes

3 (4) tablespoons Muscat de Beaumes de Venise or vin de Jura

ALTERNATIVE
CHEESES

Dolcelatte would be ideal. Even a stronger blue such as Stilton or Roquefort would work well

This may seem rather an unusual combination but, if you think about it, grapes are invariably served on a cheeseboard and they are also often cooked with quails. This recipe brings all three ingredients together. Muscat grapes are recommended for their exceptional sweetness but the dish also works well with red grapes. Serve with artichoke hearts or French beans that have been sautéed in butter with bacon and onions. If you don't manage to get hold of quails, you could use 4 poussins instead, in which case you would need to double the amount of stuffing.

Preheat the oven to 220°C, 425°F, gas 7. Season the quails inside and out. Prepare the stuffing by beating together 75g (3oz, 6 tablespoons) of the butter, the Sage Derby, shallot, garlic and a little seasoning. Stuff the quails with this mixture and seal them by pulling the skin over the opening and securing with a cocktail stick. Place in a small roasting tin. Melt the remaining butter and brush it over the quails, then roast for 12–15 minutes, until juicy and tender and still slightly pink. Remove from the roasting tin and keep warm.

For the sauce, put the quail bones in the roasting tin, place it on the hob and fry until the bones are golden brown. Add the white wine and bring to the boil, stirring to scrape up the sediment from the base of the tin. Simmer for 2 minutes, until the wine has evaporated. Pour in the meat stock and bring to the boil, skimming off any impurities from the surface. Reduce the heat and simmer for 10 minutes.

Meanwhile pass half the grapes through a centrifugal juice extractor. When the sauce has reduced and thickened to a light, syrupy consistency, strain it through a sieve into a clean pan, add the Beaumes de Venise or vin de Jura and the fresh grape juice. Simmer for 2 minutes, then add the remaining grapes to the sauce and reheat until boiling. Adjust the seasoning to taste.

Return the quails to the oven for 2 minutes to reheat them, then put them on 4 serving plates. Pour the sauce around the quails and serve.

P.G.TIPS
If you do not have a centrifugal juice extractor, purée the grapes in a liquidizer, then sieve them. If seedless grapes are unavailable, deseed them by using a clean hair grip or by cutting them in half and removing the seeds.

Roast Breast of Pheasant Wrapped in Smoked Bacon with Caraway Cabbage & Gorgonzola Polenta

SERVES 4

4 pheasant breasts, bones removed
& chopped

8 smoked bacon rashers

4 (5) tablespoons vegetable oil

75g (3oz, 6 tablespoons) unsalted butter

1 Savoy cabbage, central core removed,
finely shredded

1 teaspoon caraway seeds

300ml (½ pint, 1¼ cups) water

Freshly grated nutmeg

½ quantity of Gorzonzola Polenta
(see page 132)

Salt & freshly ground black pepper

For the sauce

3 shallots, roughly chopped

1 garlic clove, roughly chopped

1 sprig of fresh thyme

1 bay leaf

6 juniper berries, lightly crushed

6 black peppercorns, lightly crushed

5 (6) tablespoons red wine vinegar

150ml (¼ pint, ⅔ cup) red wine

150ml (¼ pint, ⅔ cup) Meat Stock
(see page 17)

4 (5) tablespoons port

½ tablespoon redcurrant jelly

I often serve this winter-inspired dish around Christmas time, garnished with baby roasted onions and glazed chestnuts – delicious! Pheasant has a tendency to be dry if not cooked with care. By wrapping the breasts in smoked bacon you can keep them moist and tender.

Preheat the oven to 220°C, 425°F, gas 7. Season the pheasant breasts all over with salt and pepper, then wrap each one in 2 overlapping rashers of bacon. Secure with a cocktail stick. Heat half the oil and butter in an ovenproof frying pan or shallow casserole dish until foaming, then add the pheasant breasts and fry briefly until browned all over. Transfer to the oven and roast for 8–10 minutes, until tender.

Meanwhile, heat the remaining oil in a saucepan and cook the cabbage over a low heat until it begins to wilt. Add the remaining butter, the caraway seeds and water. Bring to the boil and cook until the cabbage is tender and all the liquid has evaporated. Then season with salt, pepper and a little nutmeg and keep warm.

Remove the pheasant breasts from the oven and take out the cocktail sticks. Keep the pheasant warm while you make the sauce. Put the chopped pheasant bones, shallots, garlic, thyme, bay leaf, juniper berries and peppercorns in the pan in which the pheasant was cooked and fry gently for 2–3 minutes, until golden. Pour in the vinegar and boil for 1 minute, stirring to scrape up the sediment from the base of the pan. Add the red wine and boil until the liquid has reduced by half its volume. Next add the stock and boil until reduced by a third. Stir in the port and redcurrant jelly and adjust the seasoning. Strain through a fine sieve.

To serve, reheat the polenta if necessary. Arrange the cabbage on 4 warmed serving plates and place the pheasant on top. Garnish with a large scoop of polenta and pour the sauce around.

Grilled Steak Tartare with Roquefort

SERVES 4

750g (1lb 10oz) best-quality minced beef

2 tablespoons Worcestershire sauce

1 onion, very finely chopped

1 tablespoon superfine capers, rinsed, drained & chopped

1 tablespoon chopped fresh parsley

1 tablespoon Dijon mustard

1 egg yolk

150g (5oz, generous ½ cup) Roquefort, crumbled

Salt & freshly ground black pepper

ALTERNATIVE
CHEESES

For a different flavour entirely, substitute goat's cheese or Emmenthal for the Roquefort

This recipe sounds like a contradiction in terms, since the whole point of steak tartare is that it is served raw. But what I've done is taken the ingredients for steak tartare – best-quality minced beef, Worcestershire sauce, onions, capers, mustard and egg yolk – and put them together into a hamburger, with the added bonus of delicious, melting Roquefort cheese in the centre. Serve with good chunky chips and a crisp green salad.

Mix the beef, Worcestershire sauce, onion, capers, parsley and mustard together in a bowl. Season with salt and pepper, then stir in the egg yolk. Chill for about 30 minutes, until firm.

Divide the mixture into 4 balls. With your thumb, make an indentation in each one and fill with the Roquefort. Pull the meat back over the cheese until it is completely covered. Flatten into hamburgers, season lightly, then barbecue, grill or fry them.

Pepper-crusted Rib Eye of Beef with Roquefort Butter, Sautéed Potatoes & Porcini Mushrooms

SERVES 4

450g (1lb) new potatoes

4 (5) tablespoons olive oil

200g (7oz, 3½ cups) fresh porcini
mushrooms, thinly sliced

2 tablespoons roughly chopped fresh sage

4×275g (10oz) rib eye of beef steaks,
well trimmed

2 tablespoons coarsely ground
black peppercorns

½ quantity of Roquefort Butter
(see page 19)

Salt

This is a good dish for a barbecue as it can be put together very easily. However, if it rains, you can always grill or fry the steaks indoors.

Cook the potatoes in boiling salted water until just tender, then drain and leave until cool enough to handle. Peel and cut into slices 1cm (½in) thick. Heat the oil in a frying pan, add the potatoes and sauté until golden and tender. Add the porcini and sage and sauté until the mushrooms are tender. Season with salt and pepper and keep warm.

Coat the rib eye steaks evenly with the coarsely ground peppercorns and season with a little salt. Cook on a barbecue until done to your liking.

Arrange the potatoes on 4 serving plates, top with the steaks and put a pat of Roquefort butter on top of each steak. Serve immediately. The delicate cheese butter will melt on its way to the table.

P.G.TIPS

If you can't get fresh porcini mushrooms, use chestnut mushrooms instead. This simple recipe lends itself to many adaptations – for instance, lamb or pork cutlets, or a rump steak. The cheese butter is an ideal way to use up scraps of cheese.

Fillet of Beef with Bone Marrow & Parmesan Crostini & Red Wine Balsamic Vinegar Jus

SERVES 4

4×175g (6oz) fillet steaks, well trimmed (cut the trimmings into small pieces & save for the sauce)

3 (4) tablespoons vegetable oil

100g (4oz, 1 cup) mixed vegetables, such as onion, leek & carrot, finely diced

200ml (7 fl oz, scant 1 cup) red wine

4 (5) tablespoons aged balsamic vinegar

300ml (½ pint, 1¼ cups) Reduced Meat Stock (see page 17)

8 large slices of beef bone marrow (see Tip)

4×7.5cm (3in) round bread croûtes, toasted

25g (1oz, ¼ cup) fresh Parmesan, cut into shavings

Salt & freshly ground black pepper

ALTERNATIVE
CHEESE

Asiago

This dish evolved from the French classic, steak Bordelaise, which is beef in a red wine sauce with bone marrow. In my adaptation the marrow is topped with shaved Parmesan and the sauce enriched with aged balsamic vinegar. I generally serve it with buttered spinach with porcini mushrooms and pan-roasted shallots alongside, but any green vegetable would be good.

Season the steaks with salt and pepper. Heat the oil in a large heavy-based frying pan until smoking. Fry the steaks quickly on both sides so that they turn a beautiful rich dark colour, then cook until they are done to your liking: 2–3 minutes per side for rare, 5–6 for medium. Remove from the pan and keep warm in a low oven. Add the meat trimmings to the pan, together with the mixed vegetables, and fry until golden. Pour in the red wine and balsamic vinegar and bring to the boil, stirring to scrape up the sediment from the base of the pan. Boil for 5 minutes, then pour in the stock and simmer until it has thickened slightly and become syrupy; it should be thick enough to coat the back of a spoon. Taste and adjust the seasoning if necessary.

Meanwhile, poach the slices of marrow in a little salted water or, better still, meat stock for 1 minute, then drain. Put 2 slices of poached marrow on each croûte and cover with the shaved Parmesan. Put the steaks on warm serving plates, top each one with a marrow crostini and pour around the red wine sauce. Grind some black pepper over the top and serve.

P.G.TIPS You will have to go to a good old-fashioned butcher's shop to get hold of bone marrow. A very co-operative butcher might extract the marrow from the bone for you. If not, ask for bones cut into 7.5cm (3in) lengths and then poach them for 1–2 minutes. This will enable you to scoop out the marrow easily.

Veal Steaks with Blue Cheese Rarebit, Roasted Celeriac & Rosemary Sauce

SERVES 4

675g (1½ lb) celeriac, peeled & cut into batons 10×2×2cm (4×¾×¾in)

90ml (3 fl oz, ⅓ cup) vegetable oil

200g (7oz, scant 1 cup) Dunsyre Blue, finely diced

2 teaspoons mustard

100ml (3½ fl oz, ½ cup) light beer

4×150g (5oz) veal fillet steaks (or veal chops)

Salt & freshly ground black pepper

For the sauce

25g (1oz, 2 tablespoons) unsalted butter

2 shallots, finely chopped

1 tablespoon chopped fresh rosemary

150ml (¼ pint, ⅔ cup) red wine

450ml (¾ pint, 1¾ cups) Reduced Meat Stock (see page 17)

ALTERNATIVE CHEESES

Any blue such as Stilton, Beenleigh Blue or Bleu des Causses

A cheese rarebit is a peculiarly English dish that dates back at least to the time of Shakespeare. I came across this 18th-century recipe for blue cheese rarebit in an old cookery book. I like to make it with one of my favourite cheeses, Scottish Dunsyre Blue.

Preheat the oven to 200°C, 400°F, gas 6. Blanch the celeriac batons in boiling salted water for 2–3 minutes, then drain well in a colander. Place on a baking tray, toss with half the oil and bake for 20–25 minutes, until golden.

Meanwhile, for the rarebit, put the cheese, mustard and beer in a pan over a low heat, stirring constantly, until the cheese melts; the mixture should be the consistency of thickish cream. Season with pepper and keep warm.

Heat the remaining oil in a frying pan, season the steaks and fry for about 3–5 minutes on each side. Remove from the pan and keep warm.

For the sauce, add the butter, shallots and rosemary to the pan in which the veal was cooked and fry until the shallots are lightly golden. Pour in the red wine and boil for 2–3 minutes, then add the meat stock. Boil until reduced and thickened to a saucelike consistency, then strain through a fine sieve.

Spread the blue cheese rarebit over the veal steaks and place under a hot grill for 2–3 minutes, until the rarebit has turned golden and bubbly. Transfer to serving plates, pour the sauce around and garnish with the roasted celeriac.

New-look Saltimbocca

SERVES 4

4×200g (7oz) thin veal escalopes

4 slices of prosciutto

8 thin slices of fontina, rind removed

Flour, for dusting

3 eggs, beaten

75g (3oz, ¾ cup) Parmesan, freshly grated

50g (2oz, 1 cup) fresh white breadcrumbs

4 (5) tablespoons vegetable oil or clarified butter (see Tip on page 83)

2 lemons, peel & pith removed, cut into slices 5mm (¼ in) thick

Salt & freshly ground black pepper

For the sauce

300ml (½ pint, 1¼ cups) Reduced Meat Stock (see page 17)

4 (5) tablespoons Marsala wine

75g (3oz, 6 tablespoons) unsalted butter

20 small fresh sage leaves

2 tablespoons lemon juice

ALTERNATIVE

CHEESES

Port Salut or Fontal

My new-look saltimbocca uses all the elements of one of Italy's classic dishes, with the addition of thinly sliced fontina and a light Parmesan crust. In spring, asparagus tips and baby leeks make good accompaniments.

The veal escalopes should be no more than 3mm (⅛in) thick. If necessary, put them between 2 sheets of cling film and flatten with a meat mallet or a rolling pin. Season the escalopes with salt and pepper. Lay a slice of prosciutto on top of each one, then 2 slices of fontina. Fold up the edges of the veal to enclose the filling. Season again, then dust lightly with flour and chill for 30 minutes.

For the sauce, bring the stock and Marsala to the boil and simmer until it forms a light sauce consistency.

Beat together the eggs, Parmesan and breadcrumbs and add a little seasoning. Heat the oil or clarified butter in a large frying pan, dip each veal escalope into the egg and cheese mixture to coat, then fry for about 5 minutes on each side, until golden and cooked through. Transfer to a warm serving dish, top each escalope with 2 slices of lemon and pour the Marsala sauce around. Heat the butter until it is foaming and gives off a nutty aroma. Add the sage leaves and lemon juice and then pour over the veal. Serve immediately.

P.G.TIPS

It can be difficult judging the correct consistency of a sauce. If it seems too thin, reduce it by boiling until it has thickened enough to coat the back of a spoon.

Chargrilled Lamb Cutlets with Coriander & Goat's Cheese Pesto & Peppers

SERVES 4

90ml (3 fl oz, ⅓ cup) olive oil
2 garlic cloves, crushed
1 small red chilli
4 red peppers, deseeded
1 tablespoon white wine vinegar
8 thickly cut lamb cutlets (or chops)
½ quantity of Coriander & Goat's Cheese Pesto (see page 20)
Salt & freshly ground black pepper

A creamy potato purée or some soft or grilled polenta would go well with the chargrilled lamb and sautéed red peppers in this dish.

Heat the olive oil in a frying pan, add the garlic and the whole chilli and cook for 1 minute over a low heat to infuse the oil. Cut the peppers into strips 1cm (½ in) wide and add to the pan, season with salt and pepper and then sauté for 3–4 minutes. Add a little water, cover and cook over a low heat for 10–15 minutes, until tender. Uncover the pan, raise the heat and cook until all the liquid has evaporated. Add the vinegar and cook until that, too, has evaporated. Remove the chilli and adjust the seasoning. Keep warm.

Season the lamb cutlets and cook them on a ridged grill pan until they are done to your liking. Arrange the peppers on 4 serving plates, top with the lamb cutlets, then spoon over the pesto and serve.

Lamb Shanks with Feta, Anchovy & Braised Chickpeas

SERVES 6

1 tablespoon canned anchovy fillets, rinsed
2 tablespoons finely grated lemon zest
2 tablespoons chopped fresh oregano
4 (5) tablespoons olive oil
2 garlic cloves, crushed
6 small lamb shanks, trimmed
175g (6oz, ¾ cup) Greek feta
Salt & freshly ground black pepper

For the chickpeas
2 tablespoons olive oil
1 onion, finely chopped
½ tablespoon ground cumin
1 teaspoon turmeric
225g (8oz, 1⅓ cups) dried chickpeas, soaked overnight & then drained
4 tomatoes, skinned, deseeded & chopped
300ml (½ pint, 1¼ cups) tomato passata

Lamb shanks are becoming popular because they are tasty and very good value for money. Here they are served with Greek ingredients – oregano, feta, lemon and olive oil – to make a hearty and satisfying dish.

For the chickpeas, heat the oil in a pan, add the onion, cumin and turmeric and sweat until the onion is tender. Add the chickpeas, cover with water and bring to the boil. Reduce the heat and simmer for 1 hour, or until the chickpeas are tender. About 10 minutes before the end of cooking, add the chopped tomatoes and passata to form a thick sauce around the chickpeas. Season to taste.

Finely chop the anchovy fillets and mix together with the lemon zest, oregano, oil and garlic to make a paste. Rub the paste all over the lamb shanks. Leave to marinate for up to 2 hours at room temperature.

Grill the lamb on a barbecue or a ridged cast-iron grill pan for 10–12 minutes on each side (this gives pink lamb), or until done to your liking.

Meanwhile, reheat the braised chickpeas and arrange on serving plates. Top with the lamb and coarsely grate the feta over the top. Serve immediately.

CHARGRILLED LAMB CUTLETS
WITH CORIANDER & GOAT'S
CHEESE PESTO & PEPPERS

Chapter Six

Gratin of Leeks with Red Leicester & Smoked Bacon

SERVES 4

A pinch of sugar
8 medium leeks
15g (½ oz, 1 tablespoon) unsalted butter
1 tablespoon plain flour
300ml (½ pint, 1¼ cups) Vegetable Stock (see page 16) or semi-skimmed milk
1 teaspoon Dijon mustard
90ml (3 fl oz, ⅓ cup) double cream
100g (4oz, 1 cup) Red Leicester, grated
50g (2oz, ⅓ cup) smoked bacon, rind removed, coarsely chopped
Salt & freshly ground black pepper

Leeks and bacon make a wonderful marriage of flavours. With the addition of Red Leicester cheese, this simple gratin reaches new heights. It makes an ideal accompaniment to a good Sunday roast.

Bring a pan of water to the boil with the sugar and some salt. Plunge the leeks into the water and simmer for 8–10 minutes, until just tender. Remove and drain well, then dry on a cloth.

Melt the butter in a pan, stir in the flour and cook over a gentle heat for 1–2 minutes. Gradually add the stock or milk and bring to the boil, stirring constantly. Reduce the heat and cook very gently for 10 minutes. Remove from the heat and stir in the mustard, cream and half the cheese, then season to taste. Arrange the leeks in a gratin dish, season and coat with the sauce.

In a hot frying pan, sauté the bacon until crisp. Drain and scatter it over the leeks. Finally sprinkle over the remaining cheese. Place under a hot grill for a few minutes until bubbling and golden. Serve straight away.

Soft Gorgonzola Polenta with Young Spinach & Wild Mushrooms

SERVES 4-6

25g (1oz, 2 tablespoons) unsalted butter

150g (5oz, 2 cups) mixed wild mushrooms, such as ceps, chanterelles & oyster mushrooms, halved if large

90ml (3 fl oz, ⅓ cup) Madeira or port

300ml (½ pint, 1¼ cups) Meat Stock (see page 17)

2 tablespoons olive oil

100g (4oz) young spinach leaves, washed

Freshly grated nutmeg

1 tablespoon chopped fresh chives, to garnish

Salt & freshly ground black pepper

For the polenta

2 litres (3½ pints, 8¾ cups) water

2 teaspoons salt

100g (4oz, ½ cup) unsalted butter

350g (12oz, 2 cups) polenta

150g (5oz, generous ½ cup) Gorgonzola, crumbled

ALTERNATIVE
CHEESES

Bleu de Bresse or Blue Castello (Aust)

I find this creamy blue cheese polenta far superior to the plain variety finished with Parmesan.

For the polenta, bring the water, salt and butter to the boil in a large pan. Slowly rain in the polenta, stirring all the time. Simmer over a gentle heat for 30–35 minutes, stirring very frequently, until cooked; the polenta should be pulling away from the sides of the pan. Remove from the heat, stir in the Gorgonzola and allow it to melt. The polenta should be quite soft and smooth in texture. Adjust the seasoning and keep warm.

Heat the butter in a pan and fry the wild mushrooms over a high heat until tender. Remove the mushrooms from the pan and set aside. Pour in the Madeira or port and stock and boil until the liquid has reduced by half. Season to taste, return the mushrooms to the pan and keep warm.

Heat the olive oil in a pan, add the spinach and cook until just wilted, then season with nutmeg, salt and pepper.

To serve, pour the polenta into 4 warmed shallow bowls, place the spinach in the centre, then arrange the mushrooms on top. Garnish with the chives.

Aubergine & Roquefort Soufflé

SERVES 6

15g (½oz, 1 tablespoon) Parmesan, freshly grated

125ml (4 fl oz, ½ cup) olive oil

3 medium aubergines, peeled & cut into small cubes

150ml (¼ pint, ⅔ cup) water

A good pinch of paprika

75g (3oz, scant ½ cup) Roquefort

40g (1½ oz, 3 tablespoons) unsalted butter, plus extra for greasing

40g (1½ oz, ⅓ cup) plain flour

250ml (8 fl oz, 1 cup) milk, boiled & strained

4 egg yolks

6 egg whites

Salt & freshly ground black pepper

ALTERNATIVE
CHEESES

Bleu d'Auvergne, Lanark Blue, Oregon Blue (US) or Meredith Blue (Aust)

Some people find the idea of cooking a soufflé too daunting to contemplate, but as long as you follow the rules it can be a very simple dish to add to your repertoire. Here is one of my personal favourites. A delicious variation for any cheese soufflé is to put some diced cheese in the centre of the mixture when you are filling the dish. It will melt as the soufflé cooks, resulting in a wonderful fondue-like texture.

Butter six 200ml (7 fl oz, scant 1 cup) soufflé dishes or one 1.2 litre (2 pint, 5 cup) soufflé dish and dust them with the Parmesan, turning the dishes to coat them evenly. Tip out any excess cheese.

Preheat the oven to 230°C, 450°F, gas 8. Heat the olive oil in a large frying pan, add the aubergines and fry until lightly golden. Don't crowd the pan: you may have to cook them in batches. Return all the aubergines to the pan, add the water, then cover and cook over a gentle heat for up to 30 minutes, stirring occasionally, until the aubergines are very soft and fairly dry in texture. Put them in a blender with a little salt, some pepper and the paprika. To this add 50g (2oz, ¼ cup) of the Roquefort and blitz to a smooth, thickish purée. Set aside.

Heat the butter in a pan, add the flour and cook over a low heat for a few minutes. Gradually add the hot milk, stirring all the time, then bring to the boil to make a smooth sauce. Cook over a very low heat for about 5 minutes, then stir in the aubergine and Roquefort purée. Leave to cool slightly before stirring in the egg yolks.

Whisk the egg whites until they form stiff peaks. Beat a third of the whites into the sauce to loosen the mixture, then carefully fold in the remaining whites. Half fill the soufflé dishes with the mixture and crumble the remaining Roquefort over the top. Pour over the remaining soufflé mixture and wipe any drips off the rims of the dishes. Place on a baking sheet and bake for 20 minutes, until all the soufflés are well risen and nicely golden. Serve immediately.

P.G.TIPS

For successful soufflé making: ● Ensure that the bowl in which you whisk the egg whites is clean and grease free; rub it with a little lemon, then rinse under cold water and dry on a clean cloth ● Do not overbeat the egg whites or they will become grainy ● Be careful not to leave fingerprints along the rim of the soufflé dish or the soufflé will not rise evenly ● Soufflés must be served immediately. Remember: 'The guests should wait for the soufflé and not the other way round!'

Aligot
(Cheese & Potato Purée)

SERVES 4

900g (2lb) floury potatoes

175ml (6 fl oz, ¾ cup) milk, boiled
& strained

5 (6) tablespoons double cream or
crème fraîche

50g (2oz, 4 tablespoons) unsalted butter

90g (3½ oz, generous ½ cup) streaky
bacon, diced

450g (1lb, 2 cups) full-fat Tomme, such as
Cantal, cut into thin slivers

Salt & freshly ground black pepper

ALTERNATIVE
CHEESES

Although Cantal is the usual cheese,
Gruyère, Emmenthal, fontina and even
Lancashire all make good substitutes

Aligot is a peasant dish from the Auvergne region of France and makes hearty and sustaining cold-weather fare. In some areas garlic is traditionally included. It's very good served with sausages, braised meat or even, less conventionally, with fish – see the recipe for Saffron-grilled Cod Fillet with Aligot and Beurre d'Escargot on page 104.

Peel the potatoes and cook them in boiling salted water until tender. Drain well and mash until very smooth, then beat in the milk, cream or crème fraîche and butter.

In a separate pan, fry the bacon until it is crisp and the fat has been released. Add the fat (not the bacon itself) to the potato purée and season to taste. Place over a low heat and gradually fold in the cheese using a spatula. Beat the mixture; as it becomes elastic it will soften slightly and eventually be stringy when lifted with the spoon. As soon as it reaches this stage, you should serve the dish immediately.

P.G.TIPS

Aligot loses its heat fairly quickly, therefore your guests must be ready to eat it at once to appreciate it at its best. Vegetarians may omit the bacon fat.

Involtini di Melanzane al Formaggio

SERVES 4

Olive oil, for frying

2 large aubergines, cut lengthways into slices 5mm (¼ in) thick

150ml (¼ pint, ⅔ cup) tomato passata

1 ball of buffalo mozzarella, cut into slices 5mm (¼ in) thick

Salt & freshly ground black pepper

For the stuffing

100g (4oz, ½ cup) provolone, cut into small cubes

75g (3oz, generous ½ cup) pine kernels

50g (2oz, ⅓ cup) raisins, soaked in water until plump, then drained

4 (5) tablespoons olive oil

2 tablespoons fresh white breadcrumbs

1 garlic clove, crushed

2 tablespoons freshly grated Parmesan

1 tablespoon chopped fresh basil

1 egg, beaten

In my adaptation of this classic Italian dish from Campania, the aubergine slices are rolled up with a cheese, basil and raisin stuffing rather than layered in the usual way. It makes a delicious and substantial vegetarian main course.

Preheat the oven to 190°C, 375°F, gas 5. Heat a generous quantity of olive oil in a frying pan and fry the aubergine slices a few at a time until golden on both sides, adding more oil if necessary. Drain on kitchen paper and leave to cool.

For the stuffing, mix together the provolone, pine kernels, raisins, olive oil, breadcrumbs, garlic, Parmesan and basil. Season to taste and bind together with the egg. Lay out the cooked aubergine slices on a work surface and divide the stuffing between them. Roll them up fairly tightly to secure the filling and season with salt and pepper. Lightly grease a gratin dish with a little olive oil and put the aubergine rolls in it, packing them in tightly. Pour over the tomato passata and arrange the mozzarella slices down the centre. Drizzle with a little more olive oil and grind over some salt and pepper, then bake in the oven for 25–30 minutes, until golden. Cool slightly before serving.

P.G. TIPS

Although this is usually eaten hot, I was once served it cold by an Italian friend whose mother swore that it tasted better cold the next day. You know, I think I have to agree with her. Why not try it, and judge for yourself?

Courgette & Cantal Clafoutis with Rosemary

SERVES 4

2 tablespoons plain flour

3 eggs

450ml (¾ pint, 1¾ cups) milk

350g (12oz) courgettes, preferably half yellow & half green ones, cut into slices 1cm (½ in) thick

1 garlic clove, crushed

1 tablespoon chopped fresh rosemary, plus a few leaves to garnish

150g (5oz, generous ½ cup) Cantal, thinly sliced

Salt & freshly ground black pepper

ALTERNATIVE
CHEESE

Cheddar

Many people have rosemary bushes growing in their garden but only ever think to put this herb with lamb. Try it in this vegetarian dish and you'll find it partners the courgettes surprisingly well. I suggest you serve the clafoutis *as a light main course.*

Preheat the oven to 200°C, 400°F, gas 6. Beat the flour, eggs and milk together to make a smooth batter (or whizz them in a blender). Leave to stand for 20 minutes. Cook the courgettes in boiling salted water for 30 seconds, then drain well and dry them. Arrange them in overlapping circles over the base of a buttered 23cm (9in) gratin dish or flan dish and then season with salt and pepper.

Stir the garlic and chopped rosemary into the batter and pour it over the courgettes. Lay the cheese slices on top, scatter over a few rosemary leaves and bake for 30–35 minutes, until golden and well puffed up. Serve warm rather than hot. The *clafoutis* will sink before serving, so don't be alarmed.

P.G.TIPS This recipe makes a good blueprint for all sorts of variations. Try substituting butternut squash for the courgettes, or mushrooms that have been lightly sautéed with garlic, or even a combination of winter squash and mushrooms.

Winter Vegetable Pan Haggerty

4 (5) tablespoons vegetable oil

1 onion, thinly sliced

200g (7oz, 1 cup) swede, cut into fine matchsticks or coarsely grated

200g (7oz, 1 cup) turnips, cut into fine matchsticks or coarsely grated

200g (7oz, 1 cup) potatoes, cut into fine matchsticks or coarsely grated

75g (3oz, 6 tablespoons) unsalted butter, melted

75g (3oz, ¾ cup) Cheddar, grated

Salt & freshly ground black pepper

ALTERNATIVE
CHEESES

Isle of Mull or mild Parmesan

Pan Haggerty originates from Northumbria and is normally just potatoes, onions and cheese layered in a frying pan and cooked on top of the stove. My version uses a selection of root vegetables for colour and flavour and is baked in the oven rather than fried. It's good served with gammon but also makes a very nice vegetarian dish.

Preheat the oven to 200°C, 400°F, gas 6. Heat the oil in a flameproof gratin dish, add the onion and cook for 1–2 minutes, until the onions are softened but not coloured.

Drain the root vegetables separately in a colander to remove any excess moisture, then pat dry. Place a layer of swede over the onion, brush well with melted butter, season and then sprinkle on some grated cheese. Top with the turnips and more Cheddar, seasoning them and brushing with butter as before. Finally top with the potatoes, season and butter well. Add a final layer of cheese, then transfer to the oven and bake for about 45 minutes, until cooked through and lightly golden.

Turnips Stuffed with Mascarpone Creamed Spinach & Beaufort Cheese

SERVES 4

4 round turnips, about 7.5cm (3in) in diameter, peeled
50g (2oz, 4 tablespoons) unsalted butter
500g (1lb 2oz) fresh spinach
4 (5) tablespoons double cream
4 (5) tablespoons mascarpone
Freshly grated nutmeg
75g (3oz, ¾ cup) Beaufort, grated
Salt & freshly ground black pepper

ALTERNATIVE
CHEESES

Cheddar, Cantal or Gruyère

I love these simple cheese-stuffed turnips. Mascarpone is extremely rich but very good, although the first time I made the turnips I used a creamed Gorgonzola mixture. That is just as good, but, like a true chef, I enjoy experimenting with many variations. I usually serve the turnips with roast lamb, which is wonderful. Try using this stuffing in other vegetables, such as tomatoes, baby squash or artichokes.

Preheat the oven to 190°C, 375°F, gas 5. Cook the whole turnips in boiling salted water until just tender. Drain and leave to cool, then cut them in half horizontally. With a spoon, carefully scoop out the centres, taking great care to leave the sides of the turnips intact. Season the inside with salt and pepper.

Heat the butter in a frying pan, add the spinach and cook for 3–4 minutes, until it has wilted and become tender. Stir in the cream and mascarpone and season with nutmeg, salt and pepper. Fill the turnip halves with this mixture.

Place the turnip halves in an ovenproof dish and sprinkle over the grated Beaufort. Bake for 10–12 minutes, or until the cheese is browned, then serve.

Herb Cheese Sausages

SERVES 4

175g (6oz, 1½ cups) Lancashire or Cornish Yarg, grated

250g (9oz, 4½ cups) fresh white breadcrumbs, plus 100–150g (4–5oz, 2–2½ cups) for coating

2 spring onions or small leeks, finely chopped

1 teaspoon mustard powder

1 teaspoon fresh thyme leaves

1 teaspoon chopped fresh rosemary

Freshly grated nutmeg

2 eggs, separated

Flour, for dusting

Vegetable oil, for deep- or shallow-frying

Salt & freshly ground black pepper

ALTERNATIVE
CHEESES

Caerphilly, Cheddar or Cheshire

These meatless sausages from Wales are also known as Glamorgan sausages and are usually made with Caerphilly or Cheddar cheese and leeks. My favourite version uses Kirkham's Lancashire or sometimes Cornish Yarg. Serve the sausages with a tomato sauce or chutney.

Mix together the cheese, breadcrumbs, spring onions or leeks, mustard and herbs. Season with nutmeg, salt and pepper, then add the egg yolks and knead well to form a soft paste which holds its shape. Chill to firm the mixture up slightly, then shape it into 12 sausages.

Whisk the egg whites just until frothy. Dust the sausages in flour, then dip them in the egg whites and finally roll them in breadcrumbs until thoroughly coated. Deep- or shallow-fry the sausages for 3–4 minutes, or until golden, turning them occasionally. Drain on absorbent paper and serve.

Lancashire Cheese, Onion & Corn Pudding

SERVES 4

50g (2oz, 4 tablespoons) unsalted butter, plus extra for greasing

1 onion, finely chopped

1 large corn on the cob

350ml (12 fl oz, 1½ cups) milk

50g (2oz, ½ cup) plain flour

½ teaspoon mustard

125g (4½ oz, generous 1 cup) Kirkham's Lancashire, grated

Freshly grated nutmeg

4 eggs, separated

Salt & freshly ground black pepper

For the sauce

125ml (4 fl oz, ½ cup) Vegetable Stock (see page 16)

125g (4½ oz, generous ½ cup) unsalted butter, chilled & diced

2 tomatoes, skinned, deseeded & chopped

50g (2oz, ½ cup) broad beans, cooked

10 fresh basil leaves, shredded

ALTERNATIVE
CHEESES

Wensleydale or Caerphilly

This is more of a 'pudding soufflé' than a heavy pudding. Softer and quicker to ripen than Cheddar, Lancashire is the ultimate toasting cheese. Kirkham's Lancashire is the very best and, although it is usually served only on good cheeseboards, I find it hard to resist using it in cooking too.

Preheat the oven to 180°C, 350°F, gas 4. Heat 25g (1oz, 2 tablespoons) of the butter in a heavy-based pan, add the onion, then cover and sweat until tender. Shuck the corn with a knife to remove the kernels. Add them to the onion and sweat for 5 minutes, until soft. Meanwhile, chop the centre husk of the corn into small pieces and place in a pan with the milk. Bring to the boil and simmer for 5 minutes to infuse the milk, then strain.

When the corn and onion are cooked, remove from the pan. Set aside 25g (1oz, 1 tablespoon) of the corn kernels to use in the sauce. Add the remaining butter to the pan, sprinkle in the flour and stir for 1–2 minutes to form a *roux*. Pour the infused milk on to the *roux* a little at a time, blending it in well and stirring constantly to make a thick sauce. Stir in the mustard, cheese, onion and corn and season to taste with nutmeg, salt and pepper. Remove from the heat and cool slightly, then beat in the egg yolks.

Whisk the egg whites until stiff enough to hold their shape. Beat a third of the whites into the corn and cheese mixture, then gently fold in the remaining whites.

Lightly butter four 200ml (7 fl oz, scant 1 cup) soufflé dishes and fill them two-thirds full with the mixture. Place in a roasting tin containing enough hot water to come at least halfway up the sides of the dishes. Bake for 20 minutes, until risen and lightly set.

Meanwhile, make the sauce. Bring the stock to the boil in a small pan and boil for 2 minutes. Remove from the heat and whisk in the chilled butter, a few pieces at a time, to form an emulsion. Stir in the tomatoes, broad beans, reserved corn kernels and basil. Season to taste with salt and pepper.

When the puddings are done, cool them slightly before turning them out on to serving plates. Pour the sauce around and serve straight away.

P.G.TIPS
I find that eggs which are about 1 week old are best for soufflés. I've no idea why! Don't allow the cheese and corn mixture to become completely cold before adding the beaten egg whites, or the puddings will not rise to their full extent.

Potato Cakes with Ricotta & Chives

SERVES 4

675g (1½ lb) potatoes
50g (2oz, 4 tablespoons) unsalted butter
2 shallots, finely chopped
75g (3oz, ¾ cup) plain flour
1 egg
1 egg yolk
75g (3oz, ⅓ cup) firm ricotta
2 tablespoons chopped fresh chives
Freshly grated nutmeg
3 (4) tablespoons clarified butter (see Tip on page 83) or vegetable oil
Salt & freshly ground black pepper

ALTERNATIVE
CHEESES

Fresh goat's cheese or a grated hard cheese

A simple but great-tasting vegetable dish to serve with meat or fish, or even as a breakfast accompaniment. Try the potato cakes for brunch, topped with a poached egg and Hollandaise sauce as a variation on eggs Benedict.

Cook the potatoes in their skins in simmering salted water until tender, then drain well. Peel and sieve while still hot; you will need 450g (1lb, 2 cups) sieved potato. Heat the butter in a pan, add the shallots and sweat until tender but not coloured. Stir in the flour to make a thick *roux* and cook for 1 minute over a low heat. Remove from the heat, beat in the egg and egg yolk and then beat in the sieved potato, ricotta and chives. Season with nutmeg, salt and pepper and then leave to cool.

Shape the mixture into 8 potato cakes and fry in the clarified butter or oil for 4–5 minutes on each side, until golden. Serve immediately.

P.G.TIPS

You can use the potato cake mixture to make delicious gnocchi by rolling it into small balls and poaching them in boiling salted water. Put them in a gratin dish, pour a richly flavoured tomato sauce on top, and sprinkle them with grated Parmesan or Cheddar. Then brown the gnocchi under the grill.

Goat's Cheese
& Parsley Mash

SERVES 4

750g (1lb 10oz) potatoes, peeled & cut
into chunks

250ml (8 fl oz, 1 cup) milk, warmed

50g (2oz, 4 tablespoons) softened unsalted
butter

100g (4oz, ½ cup) soft goat's cheese such
as Roubiliac, sieved

2 tablespoons chopped fresh
flat-leaf parsley

Freshly grated nutmeg

Salt & freshly ground black pepper

This potato and cheese mash is particularly good served with roast or grilled chicken or lamb.

Put the potatoes in a pan of cold salted water and bring to the boil, then simmer until tender. Drain the potatoes and, while still hot, sieve them or mash well.

Beat in the warm milk and the butter, then fold in the sieved goat's cheese and parsley. Season with nutmeg, salt and pepper and serve immediately.

P.G. TIPS When it comes to preparing potato mash of any kind, I believe there is no better potato than the Desirée, with its superb dry texture and good flavour. It is well worth making the effort to find this variety.

Swede Mash with Cheddar
& Black Pepper Butter

SERVES 4

675g (1½ lb) swede, peeled & cut into
small cubes

2 tablespoons olive oil

4 (5) tablespoons milk

100g (4oz, 1 cup) mild Cheddar, grated

65g (2½ oz, 5 tablespoons) unsalted butter

1 teaspoon cracked black pepper
(see Tip)

Salt

Swede is still too reminiscent of school dinners for many people's tastes yet in the right hands it can be one of the most flavourful vegetables. Potato mashes are currently very fashionable but perhaps swede mash is the one to watch for the future! This recipe is also good when made with parsnips.

Cook the swede in boiling salted water until tender, then drain well. Purée in a blender with the oil and milk until smooth. Transfer to a clean pan and heat through, then beat in the Cheddar and 15g (½ oz, 1 tablespoon) of the butter. Season with salt to taste, then transfer to a warmed serving dish.

Melt the remaining butter with the cracked black pepper, pour it over the purée and serve straight away.

P.G. TIPS To make cracked black pepper, put some peppercorns in a small bowl and break them up roughly with the end of a rolling pin, or use a pestle and mortar.

Chapter Seven

Sambuca-flamed Ricotta with Chilled Summer Berries

SERVES 4

250g (9oz, generous 1 cup) firm ricotta

50g (2oz, ⅓ cup) caster sugar, or to taste

125ml (4 fl oz, ⅓ cup) Sambuca

100ml (3½ fl oz, ½ cup) double cream, semi-whipped

200g (7oz, 1½–2 cups) mixed berries, such as raspberries, strawberries & redcurrants, chilled

75g (3oz, ½ cup) white chocolate, cut into shavings (optional)

Sambuca is an Italian anisette liqueur. If you don't have any, you could use a fruit brandy or ordinary brandy instead. This easy dessert makes a great finale to a barbecue.

Beat the ricotta, sugar and 3 (4) tablespoons of the Sambuca together until creamy. Gently fold in the double cream and transfer to a serving bowl. Chill for at least 4 hours.

Just before serving, heat the remaining Sambuca in a small pan until very hot and pour it over the ricotta mixture. Ignite with a match; then, when the flames have died down, top with the chilled summer berries. Scatter over the white chocolate shavings, if using, and serve immediately.

P.G. TIPS

Try serving this with a fresh berry *coulis* on the side. The addition of a few toasted, flaked almonds and a little sprig of mint makes an attractive decoration and alternative to the chocolate shavings.

Rhubarb in Chilled Punch Syrup with Cheese Sorbet

SERVES 4

350ml (12 fl oz, 1½ cups) red wine

4 (5) tablespoons grenadine syrup

Juice & zest of 1 orange

1 cinnamon stick

75g (3oz, scant ½ cup) caster sugar

750g (1lb 10oz) rhubarb, peeled & cut into 5cm (2in) lengths

For the cheese sorbet

500ml (18 fl oz, 2¼ cups) milk

175g (6oz, scant 1 cup) caster sugar

Juice & zest of 1 small orange

175g (6oz, ¾ cup) cream cheese

For an interesting contrast, you could serve the rhubarb and punch syrup with the sorbet while they are still warm.

For the sorbet, put the milk, sugar, orange juice and zest in a pan and bring to the boil, stirring to dissolve the sugar, then remove from the heat and leave to cool. Stir this mixture into the cream cheese. Pour into an ice-cream maker and freeze until firm, following the manufacturer's instructions.

If you don't have an ice-cream maker, pour the mixture into a shallow container and put it in the freezer. After about 30 minutes, when the mixture is beginning to set, remove from the freezer and beat well with an electric beater or hand whisk to disperse any ice crystals, then return it to the freezer. Repeat this 2 or 3 times and then freeze until firm.

For the punch syrup, put the wine, grenadine syrup, orange juice and zest, cinnamon and sugar into a pan and boil until reduced by half its volume. Add the rhubarb to the syrup and cook gently for up to 5 minutes, until the rhubarb is tender and sweet but still holds its shape. Transfer to a bowl and leave to cool, then chill thoroughly. Serve with scoops of the cheese sorbet.

My Favourite Pick-me-up

S E R V E S 4

2 eggs

50g (2oz, ⅓ cup) caster sugar

2 tablespoons Kahlua liqueur (or Camp coffee essence)

100g (4oz, ½ cup) mascarpone

100ml (3½ fl oz, ½ cup) double cream, semi-whipped

90ml (3 fl oz, ⅓ cup) strong espresso coffee

8 boudoir sponge fingers or savoiardi, cut into 1cm (½ in) cubes

1 orange, all peel and pith removed, divided into segments, to decorate

For the orange sauce

100g (4oz, ⅔ cup) caster sugar

Juice of 2 large oranges

Zest of 1 large orange

2 tablespoons Grand Marnier

This is in fact a frozen version of that astonishingly popular dessert, tiramisù, which means pick-me-up in Italian. It is served with a refreshing orange sauce, but a plain coffee or even chocolate sauce would also be extremely good.

Put the eggs, sugar and Kahlua in a bowl set over a pan of simmering water, making sure the water is not touching the base of the bowl. Whisk until the mixture is pale, thick and creamy and has doubled in volume; a hand-held electric beater is useful for this. Remove the bowl from the pan of water and continue to whisk until the mixture is cold.

Warm the mascarpone slightly, then fold it gently but thoroughly into the mousse mixture, making sure there are no lumps. Next, gently fold in the double cream.

Put the espresso coffee in a shallow bowl and soak the sponge cubes in it for 1 minute. Take 4 metal rings, 6cm (2½ in) in diameter and 5cm (2in) high, and place them on a baking sheet. Layer the sponge fingers and mascarpone cream in the rings until they are full, then smooth the tops with a palette knife and place in the freezer for at least 3 hours, preferably overnight.

To make the orange sauce, melt the sugar in a heavy-based pan over a medium heat and stir constantly until it forms a light caramel. Carefully add the orange juice – it may splutter at first – and the zest. At this stage the mixture will crystallize; reduce the heat and cook for 2–3 minutes and the sugar will soften again. Stir in the Grand Marnier, then strain the sauce. Leave to cool and then chill until ready to use.

To serve, turn out the frozen *tiramisù* on to individual serving plates and pour the sauce around. Decorate with the orange segments.

P.G. TIPS If you don't have any metal rings you could use ramekins, although the *tiramisù* won't look as neat when turned out. In an emergency it is not unknown for chefs to use clean plastic guttering, cut into appropriate lengths!

Goat's Cheese Mousse with Pineapple Confit

SERVES 6–8

1 small pineapple

200g (7oz, 1 cup) caster sugar

300ml (½ pint, 1¼ cups) water

600g (1lb 6oz, 2¾ cups) mild fresh goat's cheese, such as Sainte-Maure or Roubiliac

200g (7oz, 1¾ cups) icing sugar

250ml (8 fl oz, 1 cup) double cream, semi-whipped

For the blackcurrant sauce

200g (7oz, 2 cups) fresh or frozen blackcurrants, plus extra to decorate

Juice of 1 orange

A little sugar, to taste

This dessert first appeared in my book Virtually Vegetarian, *but it has proved so popular and makes such good use of goat's cheese that I felt I had to include it here as well.*

Remove the outer skin of the pineapple and cut the flesh into rings, then remove the hard central core. Put the sugar and water in a pan and heat gently to dissolve the sugar, then bring to the boil to make a syrup. Add the pineapple, reduce the heat and simmer gently for about 45 minutes, until the pineapple becomes tacky and candied in appearance. Leave it to cool in the syrup. (This can be made in advance and keeps well in the refrigerator.)

Put the goat's cheese and icing sugar in a food processor and process until smooth, then transfer to a bowl. Drain the pineapple well and leave it to dry, then cut it into very small dice and add to the cheese. Gently fold in the double cream. Place the mixture in the refrigerator to firm up for at least 4 hours, or overnight.

For the sauce, put the blackcurrants in a blender with the orange juice and sugar and blitz to a smooth purée. Strain through a fine sieve.

Either serve the mousse in a single large glass bowl and hand round the blackcurrant sauce separately, or shape it into quenelles (ovals) with 2 tablespoons, arrange them on serving plates and pour the sauce around. Decorate with blackcurrants.

Goat's Cheese Ice-cream

SERVES 8

500ml (18 fl oz, 2¼ cups) milk

125ml (4 fl oz, ½ cup) double cream

4 egg yolks

1 egg

90g (3½ oz, ½ cup) caster sugar

125g (4½ oz, generous ½ cup) mild soft
goat's cheese, such as Sainte-Maure or
mild Ribblesdale

You may be surprised to see goat's cheese in an ice-cream but it gives it a delicious tanginess. The ice-cream makes a wonderful foil for cherries – try it with a warm cherry tart or clafoutis. I have included instructions for freezing without an ice-cream maker, though I believe that for fine-textured ice-creams and sorbets you do need to invest in a machine. They are quite reasonably priced now and once you have one the possibilities are endless.

Bring the milk and double cream to the boil. Whisk the egg yolks, whole egg and sugar together until thick, pale and creamy. Pour the milk and cream slowly on to the eggs, whisking all the time. Return the mixture to the pan and stir with a wooden spoon over a gentle heat until it has thickened enough to coat the back of the spoon. Do not let it boil or the eggs will scramble. Remove from the heat and stir in the cheese until it has melted into the custard. Pass through a fine sieve and leave to cool.

Pour the mixture into an ice-cream maker and freeze according to the manufacturer's instructions. If you don't have an ice-cream maker, pour the ice-cream into a shallow container and place it in the freezer. After about 30 minutes, when it is beginning to set, remove it from the freezer and beat with an electric beater or hand whisk to disperse any ice crystals, then return it to the freezer. Repeat 2 or 3 times and then freeze until firm.

Brie Ice-cream with Dates, Walnuts & Butterscotch Sauce

SERVES 8

Ingredients for the Goat's Cheese Ice-
cream (above), replacing the goat's cheese
with 125g (4½ oz, generous ½ cup)
semi-ripe Brie

150g (5oz, scant 1 cup) dates, stoned &
cut into strips

2 tablespoons walnuts, in large pieces

For the butterscotch sauce

75g (3oz, scant ½ cup) soft brown sugar

90ml (3 fl oz, ⅓ cup) double cream

75g (3oz, 6 tablespoons) unsalted butter

½ teaspoon vanilla extract

This is a shamelessly indulgent confection, rich and sticky and quite irresistible. Make sure you buy the very best quality dates, such as the succulent Medjool variety, in order to do it justice.

Remove the rind from the Brie and cut the cheese into small pieces. Make the ice-cream as for the Goat's Cheese Ice-cream and freeze until firm.

For the sauce, put all the ingredients in a heavy-based saucepan and cook over a medium heat for 3–5 minutes, stirring all the time, until the colour changes to a light caramel. Leave to cool and then chill.

To serve, put scoops of ice-cream in glass *coupes* and scatter over the dates and walnuts. Lightly coat with the chilled butterscotch sauce.

BRIE ICE-CREAM WITH
DATES, WALNUTS &
BUTTERSCOTCH SAUCE

Panna 'Ri-cotta'

SERVES 4

4 (5) tablespoons milk
150ml (¼ pint, ⅔ cup) double cream
75g (3oz, scant ½ cup) caster sugar
Zest of ½ orange
100ml (3½ fl oz, ½ cup) freshly made
strong coffee, preferably espresso
½ vanilla pod, split
2 gelatine leaves
2 tablespoons rum
200g (7oz, scant 1 cup) firm ricotta, sieved
Sprigs of fresh mint, to decorate
(optional)

For the apricot compote
75g (3oz, scant ½ cup) caster sugar
90ml (3 fl oz, ⅓ cup) water
Juice of ½ lemon
350g (12oz) fresh apricots, stoned & sliced

Panna cotta, *meaning cooked cream, is a traditional Piedmontese pudding of moulded cream lightly set with gelatine. Unconventionally, this recipe includes ricotta, so I have christened it Panna 'Ri-cotta'. Moving even further away from tradition, it is flavoured with coffee and served with a fresh apricot compote.*

Put the milk, cream, sugar and orange zest in a pan and bring to the boil. Stir in the coffee and scrape in the seeds from the vanilla pod, then add the pod as well. Remove from the heat and leave to cool. Meanwhile, put the gelatine in a small pan, cover with cold water and leave to soak for 5 minutes. Heat gently until the gelatine has dissolved.

Take the vanilla pod out of the pan and stir in the rum, sieved ricotta and the gelatine. Strain through a fine sieve, then pour into 4 ramekins or similar moulds and chill for at least 2 hours, until set.

For the compote, put the sugar, water and lemon juice in a pan and bring slowly to the boil, stirring to dissolve the sugar. Reduce the heat, add the sliced apricots and poach for about 5 minutes, until just tender. Remove from the heat and leave to cool, then chill.

Turn out the coffee ricotta custards, or serve them in the ramekins if you prefer, accompanied by the apricot compote and decorated with sprigs of mint, if liked.

Crunchy Quark Pavlovas with Caramelized Pineapple

SERVES 6

4 egg whites
225g (8oz, generous 1 cup) caster sugar
1 teaspoon vinegar
200g (7oz, scant 1 cup) quark
200ml (7 fl oz, scant 1 cup) double cream

For the Florentine
75g (3oz, scant ½ cup) caster sugar
75g (3oz, ⅔ cup) hazelnuts, chopped
75g (3oz, ¾ cup) flaked almonds

For the carmelized pineapple
100g (4oz, generous ½ cup) caster sugar
200ml (7 fl oz, scant 1 cup) water
1 small, ripe pineapple, peeled, cored &
thinly sliced into rings

In this sumptuous dessert, crushed caramelized nuts are folded into a quark and whipped cream mixture which is used to fill meringue shells. The pavlovas are then decorated with candied pineapple rings. The recipe looks quite complicated, but all the separate components can be prepared well in advance and then put together shortly before serving.

The pavlovas can be prepared a day in advance. Preheat the oven to 110°C, 225°F, gas ¼. Whisk the egg whites until they form stiff peaks and then gradually whisk in two-thirds of the caster sugar and the vinegar. Fold in the rest of the caster sugar by hand. Take 6 metal rings, 7.5cm (3in) in diameter, place them on a baking sheet and fill with the meringue (alternatively pipe it into circles on baking parchment). Carefully remove the rings and bake the meringues for 1–1½ hours, until crisp on the outside. Leave in the turned-off oven to cool.

For the Florentine, put the sugar in a heavy-based pan and melt over a medium heat, then raise the heat and cook until it is a deep golden brown. Stir in the nuts with a wooden spoon, pour the mixture on to a lightly oiled baking tray, spreading it evenly, and leave to go hard. Place the nut caramel in a small plastic bag and crush to large crumbs with the end of a rolling pin – or use a food processor.

For the caramelized pineapple, bring the sugar and water to the boil. Add the pineapple rings, reduce the heat and cook gently for about 30–45 minutes, until the pineapple becomes translucent. Leave to cool in the syrup.

Whisk the quark and cream together until thick, then fold in the crushed Florentine, retaining 50g (2oz, about 2 tablespoons) to decorate the pavlovas.

To serve, turn the meringues over and carefully scoop out the centre from the base of each one, leaving a thin shell. Fill them with the quark cream and turn right-side up again. Place on individual serving plates and decorate with the slices of pineapple. Drizzle over the pineapple syrup and sprinkle over the remaining Florentine.

Chocolate Mascarpone Brûlée

SERVES 4

425g (15oz, scant 2 cups) mascarpone
175g (6oz, scant 1 cup) caster sugar
6 egg yolks
50g (2oz) good-quality plain chocolate
Icing sugar, for dusting

This looks like a classic crème brûlée, *but when you shatter the crisp caramel topping a thin layer of dark chocolate is revealed underneath. You could put a handful of raspberries at the bottom of each dish for another unexpected treat.*

Preheat the oven to 140°C, 275°F, gas 1. Lightly whisk together the cheese, two-thirds of the caster sugar and all the egg yolks and then strain through a sieve. Pour the mixture into 4 ramekins and place them on a wad of paper in a roasting tin (the paper prevents the mixture at the bottom of the dishes getting too hot). Pour boiling water into the roasting tin to come halfway up the sides of each dish and bake for 30–35 minutes, or until the custards are just firm to the touch. Remove from the oven, take the dishes out of the roasting tin and leave to cool, then chill thoroughly.

Melt the chocolate and spread it evenly over each mascarpone custard. Return them to the refrigerator for 15 minutes so the chocolate sets hard, then sprinkle the remaining caster sugar over the top. Place under a preheated very hot grill until the sugar is golden and bubbling, then leave to cool. Dust the edges with a little icing sugar before serving.

P.G.TIPS

A very effective method is to use a small domestic blowtorch to glaze the *brûlées* instead of putting them under the grill.

Poached Figs Stuffed with Sainte-Maure Cheese in Merlot Wine Syrup

16 ripe but firm figs
100g (4oz, ½ cup) Sainte-Maure goat's cheese
50g (2oz, ¼ cup) mascarpone
Zest of 1 lemon
2 tablespoons caster sugar

For the syrup
100g (4oz, generous ½ cup) caster sugar
1 bottle of Merlot (or other red wine)
1 cinnamon stick

ALTERNATIVE
CHEESES

Any soft goat's cheese such as mild Ribblesdale or Montrachet (US). The Australian Kervella goat ricotta makes an interesting alternative

Purple figs are best for this dish. During summer I like to serve some fresh berries sprinkled around the figs.

For the syrup, put the sugar, wine and cinnamon in a saucepan that is just large enough to hold the figs in a single layer. Bring slowly to the boil, stirring to dissolve the sugar, and simmer for 4–5 minutes. Add the figs and poach for 4–5 minutes, or until just tender. Remove the figs with a slotted spoon. Boil the syrup until reduced to half its volume.

Purée 4 of the figs in a blender, adding enough of the reduced poaching syrup to give a sauce-like consistency. Strain and chill.

Beat together the Sainte-Maure, mascarpone, lemon zest and sugar. Slice the tops off the 12 remaining figs, fill with the cheese mixture and replace the tops. Arrange the figs on 4 serving plates, pour the sauce around and serve.

Pepper-caramel roasted Pears with Labna

SERVES 4

250g (9oz, generous 1 cup) live Greek yoghurt

½ teaspoon ground cinnamon

125g (4½ oz, ⅔ cup) soft brown sugar

175ml (6 fl oz, ¾ cup) water

1 cinnamon stick, broken into 3 pieces

¼ teaspoon cracked black pepper (see Tip on page 146)

4 ripe but firm Williams pears

50g (2oz, 4 tablespoons) unsalted butter

90ml (3 fl oz, ⅓ cup) Poire William or brandy

ALTERNATIVE
CHEESES

A blue cheese or curd cheese also goes well with the pears

The caramel offsets the sharpness of the yoghurt cheese, resulting in a simple dessert with complex flavours. This is really quite a straightforward recipe but you need to start preparations 3–4 days in advance, in order to drain the yoghurt for the labna.

Mix the Greek yoghurt with the ground cinnamon and then drain it through muslin for 3–4 days, as described in the recipe for Labna on page 185.

Preheat the oven to 180°C, 350°F, gas 4. Put the sugar in a heavy-based saucepan and leave over a low heat until melted. Raise the heat until it has caramelized lightly, then carefully pour in the water (the syrup may splutter) and add the cinnamon stick and cracked black pepper. Boil for 10–12 minutes to form a light syrup.

Peel the pears carefully so as to keep their shape, then cut them in half, leaving the stalks intact. Remove the cores.

Heat the butter in a large, shallow, flameproof casserole or an ovenproof frying pan, add the pear halves, flat-side down, and cook until lightly coloured. Pour over the Poire William or brandy, turn the pears over, then pour over the syrup. Transfer to the oven and bake for 40 minutes, basting the pears with the syrup once or twice to form a light glaze. Remove from the oven and cool to room temperature. To serve, top each pear half with a scoop of the labna.

Quark, Prune & White Chocolate Tart

SERVES 4–6

½ quantity of sweet pastry (see page 21)

100g (4oz) white chocolate

2 gelatine leaves

4 (5) tablespoons dry white wine

Juice & zest of 1 orange

4 egg yolks

25g (1oz, 2 tablespoons) caster sugar

125g (4½ oz, generous ½ cup) quark

150ml (¼ pint, ⅔ cup) double cream, semi-whipped

10 prunes, soaked overnight in 4 tablespoons Armagnac or brandy

ALTERNATIVE
CHEESE

Any curd cheese

Try to get really good prunes for this, preferably French Agen prunes or the large, moist Californian variety. I like to serve the tart with a fresh orange sauce, such as the one with My Favourite Pick-me-up on page 152.

Preheat the oven to 190°C, 375°F, gas 5. Roll out the pastry and use to line a 20cm (8in) tart tin. Line with greaseproof paper, fill with baking beans and bake blind for 8–10 minutes. Remove the paper and beans and bake for a further 5 minutes, then take out of the oven and leave to cool.

Melt the white chocolate in a small bowl set over a pan of hot water. Brush the base of the cooled pastry case with about two-thirds of the melted chocolate and set aside.

Cover the gelatine leaves with a little water and leave to soak for 5 minutes. Bring the wine, orange juice and zest to the boil in a pan. Whisk together the egg yolks and sugar in a bowl for 2–3 minutes, until creamy. Gradually pour the wine and orange mixture on to the yolks, whisking all the time. Cool slightly, then add the soaked and drained gelatine leaves and stir until dissolved. Fold in the remaining melted chocolate.

When the mixture is almost cold and just beginning to set, gently but thoroughly fold in the quark and the semi-whipped cream. Arrange the prunes in the pastry case, then pour in the filling. Chill for at least 2 hours for it to set.

P.G.TIPS **Don't serve the tart too cold, as this impairs the flavour. Remove it from the refrigerator and bring it to room temperature about 15 minutes before serving.**

Dried Fruit & Mascarpone Fool with Saffron & Ginger Syrup

S E R V E S   6 – 8

450g (1lb) dried apricots

600ml (1 pint, 2½ cups) water

100g (4oz, ⅔ cup) mixed dried fruit, such as apricots, prunes & figs, cut into large pieces

100g (4oz, generous ½ cup) caster sugar

Juice & zest of 1 lemon

6 (8) tablespoons apricot brandy (or orange liqueur such as cointreau or Grand Marnier)

300ml (½ pint. 1¼ cups) double cream

100g (4oz, ½ cup) mascarpone

Sprigs of fresh mint, to decorate (optional)

For the saffron & ginger syrup

2 tablespoons syrup from a jar of stem ginger

Juice & zest of 1 orange

200ml (7 fl oz, scant 1 cup) water

A good pinch of saffron strands

I devised this recipe for the Christmas edition of the BBC Vegetarian Good Food magazine, when looking for an alternative to the traditional Christmas plum pudding.

Put the dried apricots in a saucepan, pour the water over and leave to soak overnight. Bring all the ingredients for the saffron and ginger syrup to the boil, pour it over the mixed dried fruit and leave that to soak overnight too.

The next day, bring the dried apricots to the boil, then reduce the heat and simmer for 20–25 minutes until soft, adding a little more water if necessary. Transfer to a blender with the sugar, lemon juice and zest and apricot brandy and blitz to a smooth purée. Leave to cool.

Whip the cream until it is just beginning to thicken. Beat the mascarpone just to soften it and then fold it gently into the cream. Fold two-thirds of the apricot purée into this mixture. Pour the fool into tall glasses until they are almost half full. Put a spoonful of the apricot purée on top and then top up with more fool, until the mixture is 2cm (¾ in) below the rim of the glasses. Chill for 4 hours.

To serve, top up the glasses with the mixed dried fruit in syrup and decorate with the mint sprigs, if using.

Wild Loganberry & Roasted Hazelnut Cheesecake

2 eggs, separated

75g (3oz, scant ½ cup) caster sugar

225g (8oz, 1½ cups) wild loganberries, plus a few extra to decorate

2 gelatine leaves

350g (12oz, 1½ cups) full-fat cream cheese

150ml (¼ pint, ⅔ cup) double cream, semi-whipped

For the base

100g (4oz) digestive biscuits

25g (1oz, 2 tablespoons) demerara sugar

25g (1oz, ¼ cup) hazelnuts, roasted (see Tip on page 73), skinned & chopped

50g (2oz, 4 tablespoons) unsalted butter, melted

For the sauce

225g (8oz, 1½ cups) wild loganberries

Juice of 1 lemon, or to taste

Caster sugar, to taste

No book on cheese cookery would be complete without a recipe for cheesecake. I prefer the uncooked variety, so here is one of my favourites that I make at home, using autumn produce. If you can't get wild loganberries, try blackberries, blueberries or raspberries, or a mixture.

For the base, put the digestive biscuits in a food processor and blitz until they resemble coarse breadcrumbs. Transfer to a bowl and stir in the demerara sugar, chopped hazelnuts and melted butter. The mixture should be sticky but not wet. Press it firmly over the base of a 20cm (8in) springform cake tin.

Put the egg yolks and sugar in a bowl set over a pan of simmering water, making sure the water is not touching the base of the bowl. Whisk with a hand-held electric beater until the mixture is thick and creamy in colour; the beaters should leave a trail on the surface when lifted. Remove the bowl from the pan of water and leave to cool, whisking occasionally.

Purée the loganberries in a blender and then push through a fine sieve. Put the gelatine in a pan with 3 (4) tablespoons water and leave for 5 minutes, then place over a very low heat until dissolved and clear. Mix the puréed loganberries with the egg yolk mixture, then stir in the melted gelatine. Add the cream cheese and mix in thoroughly. Whisk the egg whites until stiff and fold them in. Finally, fold in the whipped cream. Pour the mixture into the cake tin and smooth the top with a palette knife. Chill for at least 2 hours, until set.

Meanwhile, make the sauce. Put the loganberries in a blender with the lemon juice and a little sugar and blitz until smooth. Pass through a fine sieve and add a little more lemon juice or sugar to taste, if necessary. Serve the cheesecake with the sauce, decorated with a few extra loganberries, if liked.

Caramelized Pastry Wafers with Blackberry Crémet

SERVES 4

200g (7oz, scant 1 cup) cream cheese or fromage frais

200ml (7 fl oz, scant 1 cup) double cream or crème fraîche, semi-whipped

2 egg whites

25g (1oz, 2 tablespoons) caster sugar

100g (4oz) puff pastry

75g (3oz, ¾ cup) icing sugar

For the blackberry purée

250g (9oz, 1½ cups) fresh blackberries

75g (3oz, scant ½ cup) caster sugar

A little lemon juice

Here, the famous crémet d'Anjou *mixture of cream and soft cheese is blended with a tart blackberry purée and served sandwiched between caramelized pastry wafers. It is quite some combination.*

Put the cream cheese or fromage frais in a bowl and beat until smooth, then fold in the whipped cream or crème fraîche. Whisk the egg whites until they form stiff peaks. Fold in the caster sugar and then fold the egg whites into the cream cheese mixture. Set aside.

Put 100g (4oz, ⅔ cup) of the blackberries in a blender, add the sugar and blitz to a purée. Transfer to a bowl and balance the sweetness with a squeeze of lemon juice. Add half the purée to the cheese mixture and gently fold it through to give a marbled effect. Cover and place in the refrigerator for about 12 hours, preferably overnight.

Preheat the oven to 220°C, 425°F, gas 7. For the pastry wafers, roll out the puff pastry in a rectangle about 15×25cm (6×10in) and approximately 2mm (1/16 in) thick. Dust with a little of the icing sugar, then roll it up very tightly like a Swiss roll. Place in a very cold refrigerator or a freezer for a short while to firm up, then with a sharp knife cut the roll into 12 slices about 5mm (¼ in) thick. (You won't need all the pastry but you can freeze the rest for later use.) Liberally dust the slices with the remaining icing sugar and roll them out as thinly as possible into ovals. Place them on a baking sheet and bake for 8–10 minutes, or until golden and caramelized. Remove from the oven and place on a wire rack to cool.

To serve, put a wafer on each of 4 serving plates and cover with some of the marbled cheese mixture. Place another wafer on top, cover with more cheese mixture, then top with a final wafer. Stir the remaining blackberries into the remaining purée and arrange around the wafer stacks.

P.G.TIPS **Pipe the cheese mixture over the pastry wafers for a professional finish. These crisp pastry wafers are also good as an accompaniment to ice-cream or sorbet. They keep for up to a week in a sealed container in a dry, cool place.**

Summer Fruit Gratin with Apricot Stilton Sauce

SERVES 4

250g (9oz, 1½ cups) fresh blackberries

50g (2oz, ⅓ cup) caster sugar, or to taste

450g (1lb, 3 cups) mixed fresh summer berries, such as strawberries, blackberries, raspberries, redcurrants

For the sauce

90ml (3 fl oz, ⅓ cup) double cream

75g (3oz, ¾ cup) white apricot Stilton, grated

2 egg yolks

50g (2oz, ⅓ cup) caster sugar

Kirsch, to taste

ALTERNATIVE
CHEESES

Any cream cheese could be substituted for the Stilton

I love the refreshing taste of these summer berries, offset with a sweet cheese sauce. Other fruit such as apricots or peaches can be used, or even poached pears during the colder months. Why not try serving the apricot Stilton sauce as a fondue for dipping fruits? In this case, a little apricot brandy may be added instead of kirsch.

Place the blackberries in a blender with the sugar and blitz to a purée. Strain the purée through a fine sieve to remove the pips. Taste and add more sugar if necessary.

For the sauce, bring the cream to the boil in a pan, then remove from the heat and stir in the cheese. Leave to cool. Put the egg yolks and sugar in a bowl set over a pan of simmering water, making sure the water does not touch the base of the bowl. Whisk until the mixture becomes pale and thick and doubles in volume. Remove the bowl from the heat and continue to whisk until the mixture is cold. Fold in the cheese and cream mixture and then add kirsch to taste.

Toss the mixed berries with the blackberry purée and pile them up in the centre of 4 heatproof serving plates. Carefully pour the cheese sauce around the fruit and put the plates under a hot grill to glaze the cheese sauce until light golden in colour. Serve immediately.

SUMMER FRUIT GRATIN WITH
APRICOT STILTON SAUCE

Lemon Blini with Ricotta & Raspberries

SERVES 4

20g (¾ oz, 1 tablespoon) caster sugar

Finely grated zest of 1 lemon

100g (4oz, 1 cup) self-raising flour

½ teaspoon baking powder

2 teaspoons melted butter

150ml (¼ pint, ⅔ cup) milk

2 eggs, separated

A pinch each of salt & sugar

1 tablespoon olive oil

4 (5) tablespoons ricotta, drained

200g (7oz, generous 1 cup) fresh raspberries

Icing sugar, for dusting

Sprigs of fresh mint, to decorate (optional)

For the sauce

250g (9oz, 1½ cups) fresh raspberries

Juice of ½ lemon, or to taste

75g (3oz, ¾ cup) icing sugar, or to taste

ALTERNATIVE
CHEESE

Quark

A simple, light, lemon-scented pancake topped with ricotta and fresh raspberries and served with raspberry sauce. I like it for dessert with a scoop of vanilla ice-cream, but it also makes an excellent brunch dish. For a winter version you could fill the blini with poached pears instead of raspberries. To make chocolate blini, replace 2 tablespoons of the flour with cocoa powder.

For the blini, mix together the sugar and lemon zest to extract the lemon's natural oils. Sift the flour and baking powder into a bowl and stir in the sugar mixture. In a separate bowl, whisk together the melted butter, milk and egg yolks, then combine with the flour to make a batter. Whisk the egg whites with a pinch of salt and sugar until they form stiff peaks, then fold them into the batter. Leave to stand for 5–10 minutes.

Meanwhile, make the sauce. Purée the raspberries in a blender, then pass them through a fine sieve. Stir in the lemon juice and icing sugar, adjusting the quantities to taste if necessary.

To cook the blini, heat the olive oil in a heavy-based frying pan over a gentle heat (or individual blini pans if you happen to have them). Then drop in 2 tablespoons of batter for each pancake so that they are about 10cm (4in) in diameter. Cook for about 2 minutes, until bubbles start to appear on the surface, then flip them over and cook the other side. Keep them warm while you cook the remaining blini – you need 8 in all.

Carefully spread the ricotta over 4 of the blini, then cover with the raspberries. Top with the other 4 blini and put on serving plates. Dust with icing sugar, pour the raspberry sauce around and serve, decorated with sprigs of mint if liked.

P.G.TIPS   I've found that American pancake and waffle mixes make a good alternative to the flour and baking powder, producing soft, light pancakes.

Corsican-style Goat's Cheese & Honey Omelette

SERVES 4

6 eggs, beaten

1 tablespoon chopped fresh mint

65g (2½ oz, ⅓ cup) caster sugar

65g (2½ oz, ⅔ cup) ground almonds

50g (2oz, 4 tablespoons) unsalted butter

75g (3oz, ⅓ cup) soft goat's cheese, such as Roubiliac, thinly sliced

2 tablespoons clear honey

Icing sugar, for dusting

Corsican food is typically Mediterranean but has a few distinctive hallmarks, one of which is the use of Broccio, a sheep's milk cheese. Broccio is popular in savoury dishes and desserts such as fritters, custards and this simple omelette. It's quite hard to obtain elsewhere, so I have substituted goat's cheese, which I actually prefer.

Put the eggs in a bowl with the mint, sugar, ground almonds and 1 tablespoon cold water and beat until light and fluffy. Heat the butter in a 20cm (8in) omelette pan. When it is foaming, pour in the beaten eggs and stir with a fork. When half set, arrange the goat's cheese slices over the top. Allow to soften slightly, then spoon over the honey and fold the omelette – or leave it flat, if you prefer. Dust with icing sugar and serve warm.

Spiced Apple & Wensleydale Pie

SERVES 4

500g (1lb 2oz, 4½ cups) cooking apples, peeled, cored & chopped

A pinch of ground cloves

1 teaspoon ground cinnamon

A pinch of freshly grated nutmeg

50g (2oz, scant ½ cup) raisins

75g (3oz, scant ½ cup) caster sugar

75g (3oz, ⅓ cup) Wensleydale cheese, broken into small chunks

½ quantity of shortcrust pastry (see page 21)

1 egg beaten with 1 tablespoon water, to glaze

Wensleydale cheese should be eaten young and fresh and is delicious with crisp autumn fruits such as apples and pears. This pie is one of my favourite old English puddings, a traditional Yorkshire way of combining apples and cheese. In this recipe the cheese is mixed with the apples for the filling, but often it is included in the pastry instead. Another Yorkshire custom is to serve a good wedge of crumbly Wensleydale with a slice of rich fruit cake or a mince pie. They both offset the cheese magnificently.

Preheat the oven to 200°C, 400°F, gas 6. Mix together the apples, spices, raisins, sugar and cheese and place in a deep 20cm (8in) pie dish. Roll out the pastry a little larger than the pie dish. Cut a thin strip from around the edge and press it on to the rim of the dish, then brush with a little of the beaten egg. Cover the pie with the pastry, pressing it on to the rim and trimming the edges. Flute the edges neatly and make a hole in the centre.

Roll out the pastry trimmings and cut out leaves or whatever shape you like. Use to decorate the pie. Brush all over with the beaten egg and bake for 15–20 minutes, until the pastry is golden. Reduce the oven temperature to 160°C, 325°F, gas 3 and bake for a further 25 minutes. Serve hot or warm, with a light custard sauce or thick clotted cream.

Hot Prune Soufflé with Goat's Cheese Ice-cream

SERVES 4
....

75g (3oz, scant ½ cup) pitted prunes,
preferably Agen prunes

40g (1½ oz, 3 tablespoons) unsalted
butter, plus extra for greasing

40g (1½ oz, ⅓ cup) plain flour

200ml (7 fl oz, scant 1 cup) milk, boiled
& strained

5 eggs, separated

2 tablespoons Armagnac

75g (3oz, scant ½ cup) caster sugar, plus
extra for dusting

15g (½ oz, 2 tablespoons) cornflour

4 scoops of Goat's Cheese Ice-cream
(see page 154)

When we were creating recipes for this book, my sous-chefs and I came across many remarkable combinations that pleasantly surprised us. None more so than this recipe pairing prune soufflé with goat's cheese ice-cream, which has turned out to be one of my favourites. Try it, and I think you'll see why.

Lightly butter 4 soufflé dishes, 200ml (7 fl oz, scant 1 cup) in capacity, and then dust with a little sugar, shaking out any excess. Preheat the oven to 200°C, 400°F, gas 6.

Simmer the prunes in water to cover until soft. Purée them in a blender and set aside. Melt the butter in a saucepan, stir in the flour and cook for 1–2 minutes. Gradually stir in the milk to form a thick sauce and simmer for 5 minutes. Stir in the prune purée, remove from the heat and leave to cool. Beat in the egg yolks and Armagnac.

Whisk the egg whites until they form stiff peaks, then gradually whisk in the sugar. Finally, whisk in the cornflour. Beat a third of the egg whites into the prune sauce and then gently fold in the rest. Pour the mixture into the soufflé dishes and put them in a roasting tin containing enough water to come two-thirds of the way up the sides of the dishes. Bake in the oven for 15–20 minutes, until well risen. Serve immediately, with the ice-cream on the side.

P.G.TIPS **A nice touch is to break open the soufflés at the table and put a scoop of the goat's cheese ice-cream in the centre of each one. You could also make extra prune purée and drizzle it over the ice-cream.**

Apple Pecorino Strudel

50g (2oz, 1 cup) fresh white breadcrumbs

50g (2oz, ½ cup) ground almonds

100g (4oz, ½ cup) unsalted butter

900g (2lb, 8 cups) cooking apples, peeled,
cored & thinly sliced

50g (2oz, ¼ cup) caster sugar

1 teaspoon ground cinnamon

½ teaspoon ground mixed spice

50g (2oz, scant ½ cup) raisins, soaked in
water until plump

25g (1oz, ¼ cup) walnuts or almonds,
chopped

Zest of ½ lemon

150g (5oz, generous ½ cup) pecorino
Romano, thinly sliced

4 large sheets of filo pastry, about
45×30cm (18×12in)

Icing sugar, for dusting

ALTERNATIVE

CHEESE

Ricotta makes a tasty alternative
to the pecorino

Another variation on the cheese and apple pie theme (see Spiced Apple and Wensleydale Pie on page 172), this time with an Italian flavour. A simple dollop of fresh cream is all you need to accompany it, but if you prefer something a little more elaborate, try a compote of plums or prunes. Strudel pastry can be time-consuming to make, but filo is generally accepted as a convenient substitute nowadays.

Preheat the oven to 200°C, 400°F, gas 6. Fry the breadcrumbs and ground almonds in 50g (2oz, 4 tablespoons) of the butter until lightly golden, then set aside.

Mix together the apples, sugar, cinnamon, mixed spice, raisins, nuts and lemon zest. Carefully fold in the pecorino cheese.

Melt the remaining butter. Lay out 1 sheet of filo dough on a work surface and brush with some of the butter, then top with the remaining sheets of filo, brushing with butter between the layers. Brush the final sheet of pastry with more butter and sprinkle the fried breadcrumb mixture over the top. Spread the apple mixture over the surface and roll up the pastry to form a compact roll. Transfer to a greased baking sheet, curving the strudel to fit if necessary, and brush with the remaining melted butter. Bake for 20–25 minutes, until crisp and golden.

Remove from the oven, dust generously with icing sugar and serve hot.

P.G.TIPS

If your filo pastry is smaller than the size given in the recipe, use extra sheets and lay them out on the work surface, overlapping the edges, to form a rectangle about 45×30cm (18×12in). Cover with a few more sheets to make 4 layers, brushing with melted butter as above.

APPLE PECORINO
STRUDEL

Cream Cheese Beignets with Walnut Honey

SERVES 4–6

450g (1lb, 2 cups) cream cheese
25g (1oz, 2 tablespoons) caster sugar
Zest of ½ lemon
150g (5oz, generous 1 cup) plain flour, sifted
2 eggs
Vegetable oil, for deep-frying
150ml (¼ pint, ⅔ cup) clear honey
75g (3oz, ¾ cup) walnuts, chopped
Icing sugar, for dusting

These beignets are one of those sticky, Middle Eastern-style desserts with lots of honey and nuts. Rather than the usual heavy pastries, however, they are light and fluffy little fritters.

Put the cheese, sugar and lemon zest in a bowl and beat together until smooth. Stir in the flour a little at a time, until thoroughly combined. Beat in the eggs one at a time, then set aside and leave to stand for up to 1 hour.

Put the vegetable oil in a deep-fat fryer or large saucepan and heat to 190°C, 375°F. Drop heaped teaspoonfuls of the cheese mixture into the hot oil a few at a time and fry for about 2 minutes, until golden and puffed up. Drain on kitchen paper and keep warm while you cook the rest.

Heat the honey and walnuts in a pan until just warm. Dust the cheese *beignets* with icing sugar and serve with the walnut honey alongside.

Cashel Blue & Pecan Pie

SERVES 4

½ quantity of sweet pastry (see page 21)
Flour, for dusting
65g (2½ oz, 5 tablespoons) unsalted butter
4 (5) tablespoons golden syrup
100g (4oz, ½ cup) Cashel Blue or similar mild blue cheese, cut into small cubes
150g (5oz, ⅔ cup) soft brown sugar
3 eggs
2 tablespoons rum
½ teaspoon vanilla extract
A pinch of salt
150g (5oz, generous 1 cup) pecan nuts

ALTERNATIVE

CHEESE

If you prefer a stronger cheese, you could use Roquefort or Gorgonzola

Pecan pie is virtually America's national dessert. The addition of blue cheese makes an interesting variation. I like to serve the pie warm with lashings of double cream.

Preheat the oven to 190°C, 375°F, gas 5. Roll out the pastry on a lightly floured surface until it is 3mm (⅛in) thick and use to line a 23cm (9in) flan tin, 2.5cm (1in) deep. Prick the base with a fork, line with greaseproof paper and fill with baking beans. Bake blind for 10 minutes, then remove the paper and beans and bake for a further 5 minutes. Remove from the oven and reduce the temperature to 180°C, 350°F, gas 4.

Heat the butter and golden syrup in a pan, add half the cheese and stir until melted. In a bowl, whisk together the sugar, eggs, rum, vanilla and salt. Add the pecan nuts and then stir into the syrup and cheese mixture. Add the remaining cheese and pour the mixture into the pastry case. Bake for about 30 minutes, until just set.

CASHEL BLUE
& PECAN PIE

Croque Mademoiselle

SERVES 4

90g (3½ oz, scant ½ cup) Neufchâtel

1 tablespoon Grand Marnier

Zest of ½ orange

3 tablespoons caster sugar

8 slices of brioche (see page 22), crusts removed

250g (9oz, 1½ cups) raspberries

2 eggs, beaten

150ml (¼ pint, ⅔ cup) double cream

150ml (¼ pint, ⅔ cup) milk

1 teaspoon ground cinnamon

50g (2oz, 4 tablespoons) unsalted butter

Icing sugar, for dusting

ALTERNATIVE
CHEESES

If Neufchâtel is too strong for your taste, replace it with quark or firm ricotta

Made with Neufchâtel cheese, this delicate, sweet version of croque monsieur is not unlike pain perdu, or French toast. Although it can be served for dessert, it also makes a good brunch dish or summer breakfast. Neufchâtel is a creamy, fresh-tasting cheese from Normandy, best eaten young.

Mix together the Neufchâtel, Grand Marnier, orange zest and 1 tablespoon of the sugar. Spread this mixture evenly over the slices of brioche. Top 4 slices with the raspberries, packing them tightly into the cheese, then sandwich together with the remaining brioche.

Beat together the eggs, cream, milk, cinnamon and remaining sugar and pour into a shallow dish. Dip the sandwiches into this mixture on both sides. Heat the butter in a large frying pan and cook the sandwiches for about 2 minutes on each side, until golden. Remove and drain on kitchen paper, then dust liberally with icing sugar. Serve the *Croques Mademoiselles* immediately, with some lightly whipped cream.

P.G.TIPS You could substitute white bread for the brioche, although the flavour won't be quite as good. Some supermarkets stock light toast breads, which would work better than plain white bread.

Tourte de Poitou

SERVES 6

½ quantity of sweet pastry (see page 21)

Flour, for dusting

175g (6oz, ¾ cup) soft, unsalted goat's cheese, such as Sainte-Maure

3 eggs

100g (4oz, generous ½ cup) caster sugar

2 tablespoons double cream

3 (4) tablespoons finely chopped candied fruit

Zest of 1 orange

1 tablespoon pistachio nuts, skinned & chopped (see Tip)

This tart is a speciality of the Poitou region in France, where it is made with goat's cheese, as below. You could substitute cream cheese, if you prefer.

Preheat the oven to 190°C, 375°F, gas 5. Roll out the pastry on a lightly floured surface until it is 3mm (⅛ in) thick and use to line a 20cm (8in) flan tin. Prick the base with a fork, line with greaseproof paper and fill with baking beans. Bake blind for 10 minutes, then remove the paper and beans and return to the oven for 5 minutes longer.

Meanwhile, beat together all the remaining ingredients in a bowl until thoroughly combined. Pour into the pastry shell and return to the oven to bake for 45 minutes, until the top is a deep golden brown. Serve warm or, if you prefer, cold.

P.G.TIPS To skin pistachio nuts, put them on a baking tray in a fairly hot oven for 1–2 minutes, then place them in a clean tea towel and rub gently to loosen the skins. Leave to cool, then peel off the skins.

Baked Amaretti Peaches with Ricotta & Bitter Chocolate

SERVES 4

300ml (½ pint, 1¼ cups) dry white wine

4 (5) tablespoons Amaretto liqueur (optional)

100g (4oz, generous ½ cup) caster sugar

½ teaspoon vanilla extract or 1 vanilla pod, split open

4 large, ripe peaches

4 (5) tablespoons firm ricotta

50g (2oz, 1 cup) amaretti biscuits, crushed into small pieces

2 tablespoons grated bitter chocolate (use plain chocolate with at least 70% cocoa solids)

2 tablespoons semi-whipped double cream

Fillings for baked peaches are legion, but this combination of soft, fresh cheese, bitter chocolate and almond biscuits is especially good. Apricots can be prepared in the same way.

Preheat the oven to 220°C, 425°F, gas 7. Bring the wine, Amaretto liqueur, if using, sugar and vanilla to the boil in a pan and boil for 5 minutes to form a light syrup. Add the peaches and poach for 1 minute. Remove the peaches with a slotted spoon and drain well, then slip off their skins. Cut the peaches in half, following the indentation that runs around their circumference. Twist each peach to loosen both halves and then remove the stone. Using a teaspoon, carefully scoop out a little of the flesh to enlarge the cavity.

In a bowl, mix together the ricotta, crushed amaretti and chocolate, then fold in the cream. Fill the peach halves with this mixture and place them in a baking dish that is just large enough to hold them in a single layer. Pour a little of the poaching syrup into the dish around the peaches and bake for 5–8 minutes, until golden. Serve immediately, with a good vanilla ice-cream.

P.G.TIPS

Freeze any leftover poaching syrup to make a delicately flavoured peach sorbet. An ideal way to enjoy this dessert all year round is to buy your peaches in the summer and bottle them in syrup for storing. They are also delicious served in their syrup with vanilla ice-cream.

Cretan Sheep's Milk Turnovers with Melted Honey

SERVES 4

125g (4½ oz, generous ½ cup) Greek feta

40g (1½ oz, scant ¼ cup) cream cheese

1 egg, beaten

50g (2oz, 4 tablespoons) softened unsalted butter

¼ teaspoon ground cinnamon

Juice of ¼ lemon

2 tablespoons chopped fresh mint

Vegetable oil, for deep-frying

Icing sugar, for dusting

150ml (¼ pint, ⅔ cup) honey, warmed

150ml (¼ pint, ⅔ cup) crème fraîche (optional)

For the pastry

225g (8oz, 2 cups) plain flour, plus extra for dusting

25g (1oz, 2 tablespoons) caster sugar

25g (1oz, 2 tablespoons) unsalted butter at room temperature, diced

About 150ml (¼ pint, ⅔ cup) water

This marriage of sweet and salty flavours is common in Mediterranean countries. I like to serve some crème fraîche with the turnovers, which makes for a nice contrast of temperatures.

To make the pastry, sift the flour into a bowl, stir in the sugar, then rub in the butter pieces with your fingertips to give a coarse, sandy texture. Stir in enough water to make a soft, pliable dough. Turn out on to a lightly floured work surface and knead for 4–5 minutes, until smooth and elastic.

Place the feta in a bowl and crush it to a coarse pulp with a fork. Add the cream cheese and egg and beat together until smooth. Next, beat in the butter and cinnamon, then the lemon juice and chopped mint. Set aside in the refrigerator until required.

Roll the pastry out as thinly as possible on a lightly floured surface. Cut out 16–20 rounds with a 7.5cm (3in) pastry cutter. Put about 1 tablespoon of the feta filling on one half of each pastry round, brush the edges with water, then fold over and seal well to make turnovers. Place them in the refrigerator for 30 minutes to firm up.

Meanwhile, pour the vegetable oil into a deep-fat fryer or a deep saucepan and heat to 180–190°C, 350–375°F. Carefully slip the turnovers into the hot oil, a few at a time, and cook for about 2 minutes or until golden, turning them occasionally. Take out and drain on kitchen paper to remove excess oil. Keep warm while you fry the remaining turnovers.

Place the turnovers on a serving dish, sift over a little icing sugar and drizzle with warm melted honey. Serve immediately, with crème fraîche if you like.

P.G. TIPS

Try to find a good Greek honey to use in this recipe. If time is of the essence, you could try using filo pastry instead. The result will be almost as good, although the turnovers will be a little crispy.

Chapter Eight

Pressed Cheese with Dried Fruits

SERVES 4

4 crottin de Chavignol or aged Chabis goat's cheeses, cut horizontally in half

50g (2oz, ⅓ cup) dried figs, cut into quarters

50g (2oz, ¼ cup) prunes, cut in half

3 sprigs of fresh thyme

3 bay leaves

6 black peppercorns

6 (8) tablespoons prune eau de vie or cognac

Olive oil

Serve this delicious cheese preserve with a good walnut bread.

Place 2 of the cheese halves in a sterilized 500ml (18 fl oz, 2¼ cup) preserving jar and scatter over a third each of the figs and prunes, plus a sprig of thyme, a bay leaf and 2 peppercorns. Sprinkle over 1½ tablespoons of the eau de vie or cognac. Put 2 more cheese halves on top and repeat these layers until all the ingredients are used up, ending with a layer of cheese and pressing it down well. The cheese should be tightly packed. Sprinkle over the remaining eau de vie or cognac. Pour in enough olive oil to cover the cheese and then leave in a cool place, but not the refrigerator, for at least a week. Store in the refrigerator once opened.

Simple Marinated Chèvre in Basil Oil

SERVES 4

4 crottin de Chavignol or aged Chabis
goat's cheeses, cut horizontally in half

1 bay leaf

6 black peppercorns, lightly crushed

2 garlic cloves, crushed

1 handful of fresh basil leaves

125ml (4 fl oz, ½ cup) extra-virgin
olive oil, warmed

Salt

ALTERNATIVE
CHEESES

A creamy Camembert or Brie,
cut into slices 1cm (½ in) thick,
or Roubiliac goat's cheese balls

A quick and simple method of marinating cheese, with basil, olive oil and garlic. I like to serve it as part of a cheeseboard but it also makes a good light starter accompanied by a small crisp salad and some bread.

Place the cheese halves in a dish just large enough to hold them in one layer and put the bay leaf and peppercorns on top. Blitz the garlic, basil and olive oil together in a blender to form a fairly liquid sauce and then season with salt. Pour the basil oil over the cheese, cover and leave in a cool place for about 6 hours. It will keep for about a week in the refrigerator, but bring to room temperature before serving.

Stuffed Bonchester with Walnuts

SERVES 4

1 Bonchester, not too ripe

65g (2½ oz, ⅓ cup) fresh goat's cheese,
such as Sainte-Maure

25g (1oz, 2 tablespoons) softened
unsalted butter

40g (1½ oz, ⅓ cup) walnuts, chopped

3 (4) tablespoons double cream

Salt & freshly ground black pepper

ALTERNATIVE
CHEESES

Brie or Coulommiers (you will need to
double the filling ingredients if you use
these) or Camembert

This was a popular idea in France when nouvelle cuisine *was in vogue. Some Michelin-starred restaurants would serve a Brie that had been stuffed with a mixture of soft cheese and fresh truffles. This cheaper variation uses walnuts but you could, of course, replace them with truffles.*

Slice the Bonchester in half horizontally. Beat together the goat's cheese, butter, walnuts and cream and season with salt and pepper. Spread this mixture over the cut sides of the cheese and then sandwich them together. Chill in the refrigerator for 2 hours to firm up the filling and then cut into small wedges to serve.

P.G.TIPS

Using a hot carving knife to slice the Bonchester will make the job easier. The stuffed Bonchester is particularly delicious served with ripe, fresh figs.

Liptauer

SERVES 4

225g (8oz, 1 cup) cream cheese, such as Philadelphia or fresh Explorateur

4 (5) tablespoons soured cream

50g (2oz, 4 tablespoons) softened unsalted butter

2 teaspoons superfine capers, drained

2 canned anchovy fillets, finely chopped

1 tablespoon chopped fresh chives

1 tablespoon mild paprika, plus extra for dusting

1 teaspoon caraway seeds

½ teaspoon mild mustard

Salt

This cheese dip from Hungary is usually made from a soft sheep's milk cheese, which is not always easy to obtain, so I have substituted cream cheese. Crisp biscuits are great with this, although a selection of vegetable crudités is also very good. Liptauer *keeps for about a week in the refrigerator.*

Blend all the ingredients together briefly in a food processor or beat them together in a bowl. Cover and leave overnight in the refrigerator to allow the flavours to infuse. To serve, adjust the seasoning if necessary, transfer to a serving dish and dust the top with a little paprika.

Labna with Oregano & Paprika Oil

SERVES 4

500g (1lb 2oz, 2¼ cups) live Greek yoghurt

6 large sprigs of fresh oregano

About 600ml (1 pint, 2½ cups) olive oil

1 tablespoon paprika

Labna, also known as dry yoghurt cheese, is popular throughout the Middle East and can be prepared very simply at home by draining yoghurt through muslin. It makes a useful base for savoury or sweet dishes (see the recipe for Pepper-caramel-roasted Pears on page 162) or can be rolled into balls and preserved in oil, as here. If the labna *is too acidic for your taste, try stirring in a tablespoon of lightly whipped double cream.*

Line a colander with 4 layers of dampened muslin. Pour in the yoghurt, then tie together the ends of the muslin and hang it up over a bowl. Leave to drain in a cool place such as an unheated room for 3–4 days. On hot days, you may need to drain it in the refrigerator.

Unwrap the yoghurt cheese and roll it into small balls, about 2.5cm (1in) in diameter. Place them in a sterilized preserving jar, tucking in the sprigs of oregano. Mix the oil with the paprika and pour it over the cheese; make sure it is completely covered. Close the preserving jar and leave in a cool place for at least a week before using. Serve with crusty bread.

Gooseberry & Green Peppercorn Chutney

MAKES about 900g (2lb)

600g (1lb 6oz, about 3½ cups) fresh green or red gooseberries

2 onions, chopped

1 garlic clove, crushed

½ teaspoon mustard powder

1 teaspoon lemon juice

300ml (½ pint, 1¼ cups) cider vinegar or white wine vinegar

175g (6oz, generous 1 cup) raisins

75–275g (3–10oz, ½–1½ cups) soft brown sugar

A large pinch of salt

2 tablespoons green peppercorns

Serve this chutney with a selection of cheeses and some crusty bread. If you are using the sweeter red gooseberries, you will need the smaller amount of sugar listed in the ingredients. Although you can store it in preserving jars for months, a good chutney will also keep for one month unsealed in the refrigerator and will, in fact, improve in flavour.

Put the gooseberries, onions, garlic, mustard and lemon juice in a preserving pan and pour over two-thirds of the vinegar. Bring to the boil, then reduce the heat and simmer for about 45 minutes, stirring occasionally, until thick. Add the raisins, salt, sugar and the rest of the vinegar. Stir over a low heat until the sugar has dissolved, then simmer for up to 1 hour, stirring frequently, until thick and syrupy. Stir in the peppercorns, then remove from the heat. Either leave to cool, then store in the refrigerator for up to a month, or pour immediately into hot sterilized jars, seal and store in a cool, dark place.

Saffron Pear Chutney

MAKES about 900g (2lb)

2 cooking apples, peeled & grated

125g (4½ oz, scant 1 cup) onions, finely chopped

125g (4½ oz, generous ⅔ cup) sultanas

Juice & zest of 4 oranges

300g (11oz, 1½ cups) granulated sugar

1 teaspoon ground cinnamon

1 teaspoon freshly grated nutmeg

1 teaspoon cayenne pepper

2 pinches of saffron strands

1½ teaspoons salt

50g (2oz, 4 tablespoons) fresh ginger root, grated

300ml (½ pint, 1¼ cups) white wine vinegar

750g (1lb 10oz, 6½ cups) pears, peeled, cored & roughly chopped

350g (12oz, 2½ cups) tomatoes, skinned, deseeded & diced

The pears are cooked quite briefly so that they keep their shape, resulting in a nice chunky chutney. It is very good served with a mature farmhouse Cheddar such as Montgomery's or Keen's.

Put all the ingredients except the pears and tomatoes in a preserving pan and simmer for about 30 minutes, stirring from time to time, until the mixture is reduced to a syrup. It should be thick enough to coat the back of a spoon. Add the pears and tomatoes and cook for 10–15 minutes, until the pears are just soft. Pour into hot sterilized jars and seal, then store in a cool, dark place.

CHEESEBOARD (clockwise from top): CAPRICORN, SAINTE-MAURE, KEEN'S CHEDDAR, GOLDEN CROSS, BOULETTES D'AVESNES, ROQUEFORT SOCIETÉ, REBLOCHON

Sweet & Sour Grape Pickle

MAKES about 1 litre

(1 ¾ pints, 4 cups)

750g (1lb 10oz, about 4½ cups) seedless white grapes

10 sprigs of fresh tarragon

500ml (18 fl oz, 2¼ cups) champagne vinegar or white wine vinegar

175ml (6 fl oz, ¾ cup) honey

1 teaspoon salt

A delicately flavoured pickle that makes an interesting accompaniment to cheese. Although this recipe uses white grapes, you could substitute red ones. Remember that good-quality vinegar is essential for making a good pickle.

Wash the grapes well and then dry them. Put them in a large sterilized preserving jar with the sprigs of tarragon. Boil the vinegar and honey together for 2 minutes, then add the salt and pour the mixture over the grapes. Seal the jar immediately. For best results, store in a cool dark place for up to 1 month before opening.

Lanesborough Dried Fig & Fennel Seed Bread

MAKES 1 LOAF

15g (½ oz) fresh yeast or ½ sachet Easyblend yeast

125ml (4 fl oz, ½ cup) water

250g (9oz, scant 2 cups) strong brown flour

½ teaspoon salt

15g (½ oz, 1 tablespoon) unsalted butter

150g (5oz, scant 1 cup) dried figs, cut into strips about 5mm (¼ in) wide

1½ teaspoons fennel seeds

This delicately flavoured loaf is one of my favourites and a real winner at the Lanesborough, where we serve it as an accompaniment to our cheese selection. I like it slightly warm with my cheese.

If using fresh yeast, put it in a small bowl, pour on the water and mix until smooth. Sift the flour and salt into another bowl and rub in the butter, then make a well in the centre and add the yeast and water mixture. Stir in the flour to form a soft dough. If using Easyblend yeast, stir it into the flour after rubbing in the butter and then pour in the water.

Turn the dough out on to a lightly floured surface and knead for 8–10 minutes, until smooth and elastic. Add the dried figs and fennel seeds and knead for 1 minute longer, until incorporated. Do not overknead the dough at this stage or the figs will disintegrate. Leave to relax for about 5 minutes, then shape into an oval loaf, place on a greased baking sheet and cover with a clean damp tea towel. Leave in a warm place for about 50 minutes, until it has doubled in size.

Preheat the oven to 220°C, 425°F, gas 7. Bake the loaf for 30 minutes, or until it is golden brown on top and sounds hollow when tapped underneath. Cool on a wire rack.

BREADS (clockwise from top): STILTON BREAD, MOZZARELLA & SUN-DRIED TOMATO BREAD, LANESBOROUGH DRIED FIG & FENNEL SEED BREAD, CHEDDAR & ONION LOAF, CHEDDAR & ONION LOAF, STILTON BREAD (centre)

INDEX

aligot (cheese and potato purée), 135
apples: apple pecorino strudel, 174
    spiced apple and Wensleydale pie, 172
artichokes, Greek-style baked, 44
Asiago, baked walnut gnocchi with
    Gruyère and, 97
asparagus risotto with fonduta, 96
aubergines: aubergine and Roquefort
    soufflé, 134
    involtini di melanzane al formaggio, 136
    roasted aubergine *moutabel*, 36

Beaufort, turnips stuffed with mascarpone
    creamed spinach and, 141
beef: carpaccio of beef, 48
    fillet with bone marrow and Parmesan
    crostini, 124
    grilled steak tartare, 121
    pepper-crusted rib eye of beef, 122
Beenleigh Blue, pear and rosemary
    galettes, 38
Bel Paese *calzoni*, 90
beurre d'escargot, 104
Bleu d'Auvergne: glazed oysters on
    crushed potatoes with, 30
    wine-roasted turbot with, 108
blue cheeses, 12
Bonchester, stuffed with walnuts, 184
Boursin: baked bucatini with garlic cheese
    and ricotta sauce, 84
bread: bread and Pecorino soup, 64
    Cheddar and onion loaf, 22
    Italian picnic loaf, 23
    Lanesborough dried fig and fennel seed
    bread, 188
    Stilton bread, 23
Brie ice-cream, 154
brioche, 22
    croque Mademoiselle, 178
    Parmesan brioche toast, 32
    warm brioche of goat's cheese, 40
bucatini baked with garlic cheese and
    ricotta sauce, 84
butters, cheese, 19

cabbage: baked Reblochon in, 42
    white cabbage and oyster broth with
    Fourme d'Ambert, 55
Cabécou-stuffed tomatoes, 58
calzoni, 90
Camembert: Camembert butter, 19

French onion soup with, 64
    melting Camembert fritters, 47
    mussel fondue Normandie, 114
    wing of skate with, 106
cannellini bean soup, 56
Cantal: *aligot* (cheese and potato
    purée), 135
    courgette and Cantal *clafoutis*, 138
    potato and Cantal soup, 54
caramelized pastry wafers, 167
Cashel Blue: Cashel Blue and pecan
    pie, 176
    pressed leek terrine with, 29
cauliflower cheese soup, 60
Cheddar: cauliflower cheese soup, 60
    Cheddar and onion loaf, 22
    lobster and Gospel Green Cheddar
    bisque, 62
    swede mash with, 146
    winter vegetable Pan Haggerty, 140
cheese-making, 9
cheeseboards, 12–13, 183
cheesecake, wild loganberry and roasted
    hazelnut, 166
chicken: chicken schnitzel with
    mozzarella, 115
    grilled chicken spatchcock, 116
    stocks, 16, 17
chilli-pickled orange, feta and olive
    salad, 76
chocolate mascarpone *brûlée*, 159
chutneys, 186
cod fillet, saffron-grilled, 104
coffee: my favourite pick-me-up, 152
    panna 'ri-cotta', 156
coriander and goat's cheese pesto, 20
cottage cheese: Topfenravioli, 86
courgettes: courgette and Cantal
    clafoutis, 138
    crisp, flowering courgettes with
    mozzarella and anchovy, 46
crab and asparagus salad, 74
cream cheese: caramelized pastry wafers
    with blackberry crémet, 167
    cheese sorbet, 150
    cream cheese beignets, 176
    Liptauer, 185
    taramasalata with cream cheese, 25
    wild loganberry and roasted hazelnut
    cheesecake, 166
croque Mademoiselle, 178

dolcelatte: carpaccio of beef with
    dolcelatte mustard dressing, 48
    oyster and spinach pizza with, 92
    pennette al dolcelatte, 88
    stuffed macaroni *al forno* with Swiss
    chard and Italian cheeses, 85

dried fruits: dried fruit and mascarpone
    fool, 164
    pressed cheese with, 183

eggs: Corsican-style goat's cheese and
    honey omelette, 172
    tagliatelle with fried egg, capers and
    pecorino Sardo, 83
Emmenthal: Emmenthal *corniottes*, 28
    Emmenthal floating islands, 52
    flamiche aux trois fromages, 41
    mussel fondue Normandie, 114

feta: chilli-pickled orange, feta and olive
    salad, 76
    Cretan sheep's milk turnovers, 180
    feta and roasted pepper mousse, 28
    lamb shanks with, 128
figs: Lanesborough dried fig and fennel
    seed bread, 188
    poached figs stuffed with Sainte-Maure
    cheese, 160
fish and seafood, 101–14
flamiche aux trois fromages, 41
fondues: mussel fondue Normandie, 114
fontina: asparagus risotto with *fonduta*, 96
    cannellini bean soup with fontina
    gremolata, 56
    crispy cheese risotto *al salto*, 97
    insalata di fontina, 79
    new-look *saltimbocca*, 126
fool, dried fruit and mascarpone, 164
Fourme d'Ambert, white cabbage and
    oyster broth with, 55
fritters, 47, 94
fruit: Sambuca-flamed ricotta with chilled
    summer berries, 149
    summer fruit gratin, 168

gazpacho, tomato, 58
Glamorgan sausages, 142
gnocchi, baked walnut, 97
goat's cheeses, 11–12
    baked Reblochon in Savoy cabbage, 42
    Cabécou-stuffed tomatoes, 58
    chargrilled lamb cutlets with goat's
    cheese pesto, 128
    coriander and goat's cheese pesto, 20
    Corsican-style goat's cheese and honey
    omelette, 172
    flamiche aux trois fromages, 41
    goat's cheese and cumin vinaigrette, 20
    goat's cheese and parsley mash, 146
    goat's cheese ice-cream, 154, 173
    goat's cheese mousse, 153
    marinated chèvre in basil oil, 184
    plum tomato salad with goat's milk
    dressing, 67

poached figs stuffed with Sainte-Maure cheese, 160
pressed cheese with dried fruits, 183
rigatoni with mixed peppers and coriander and goat's cheese pesto, 88
roasted aubergine *moutabel* with Roubiliac and thyme, 36
roasted vegetable pizza with, 91
saffron vegetable chowder with coriander and goat's cheese pesto, 65
stuffed Bonchester with walnuts, 184
tourte de Poitou, 178
warm brioche with minted leeks, 40
warm lentil salad with pepper-grilled goat's cheese and anchovy toasts, 70
Golden Cross: *flamiche aux 3 fromages*, 41
gooseberry and green peppercorn chutney, 186
Gorgonzola: kohlrabi and Gorgonzola soup, 61
roast breast of pheasant with caraway cabbage and Gorgonzola polenta, 120
soft Gorgonzola polenta, 132
suppli alla Gorgonzola con basilico, 94
goyère, 37
grape pickle, sweet and sour, 188
Gruyère: baked walnut gnocchi with, 97
basic cheese sauce (sauce Mornay), 18

haloumi, twice-roasted red peppers with capers, olives and, 26
hard cheeses, 9–10
herb cheese sausages, 142
herrings, salad of pickled, 72

ice-cream: Brie, 154
goat's cheese, 154
insalata di fontina, 79
involtini di melanzane al formaggio, 136
Italian picnic loaf, 23

Jarlsberg, salad of pickled herrings, potatoes, dill and, 72

kasseri: Greek-style baked artichokes with coriander, mint and lemon, 44
kohlrabi and Gorgonzola soup, 61

labna: with oregano and paprika oil, 185
pepper-caramel roasted pears with, 162
lamb: chargrilled lamb cutlets, 128
lamb shanks with feta, 128
salad of grilled lamb fillet, 80
Lanark Blue: salad of grilled lamb fillet with, 80
Lancashire: herb cheese sausages, 142
Lancashire cheese, onion and corn pudding, 144

Lanesborough dried fig and fennel seed bread, 188
leeks: blackened leek, red onion and smoked mozzarella salad, 68
gratin of leeks, 131
pressed leek terrine, 29
warm brioche of goat's cheese with, 40
lemon blini with ricotta, 170
lentil salad, warm, 70
Liptauer, 185
lobster: gratin of lobster, 110
lobster and Gospel Green Cheddar bisque, 62
loganberry and roasted hazelnut cheesecake, 166

macaroni al forno, 85
malfattini of ricotta and rocket, 98
Manchego, sizzling prawns with, 112
Maroilles: *goyère*, 37
mascarpone: chocolate *brûlée*, 159
dried fruit and mascarpone fool, 164
my favourite pick-me-up, 152
turnips stuffed with mascarpone creamed spinach, 141
mayonnaise, quark, 21
meat stock, 17
meringue, 158
mousses, 28, 153
mozzarella: blackened leek, red onion and smoked mozzarella salad, 68
chicken schnitzel with, 115
crisp, flowering courgettes with, 46
involtini di melanzane al formaggio, 136
ratatouille-stuffed, 34
red mullet on baked salad caprese, 101
ultimate vegetarian *calzoni*, 90
mushrooms, Gorgonzola polenta with, 132
mussel fondue Normandie, 114
my favourite pick-me-up, 152

Neufchâtel: *croque Mademoiselle*, 178

omelettes *see eggs*
onion soup, French, 64
orange, feta and olive salad, chilli-pickled, 76
oysters: glazed oysters on crushed potatoes, 30
oyster and spinach pizza, 92

Pan Haggerty, winter vegetable, 140
panna 'ri-cotta', 156
Parmesan: Cornish crab and asparagus salad, 74
fillet of beef with bone marrow and Parmesan *crostini*, 124
gratin of lobster with, 110

new-look *saltimbocca*, 126
Parmesan brioche toast, 32
Parmesan-crusted sea bass, 102
rapid cheese sauce, 18
stuffed sardines with Parmesan gremolata and caper butter, 109
zuppa Pavese, 54
pasta, 83–8
pasta filata cheeses, 11
pastry, 21
pavlovas, crunchy quark, 158
pea and watercress soup, 52
peaches, baked amaretti, 179
pears: pear, Beenleigh Blue and rosemary galettes, 38
pear, celeriac and Stilton vichyssoise, 51
pepper-caramel-roasted pears, 162
saffron pear chutney, 186
pecan pie, 176
pecorino: apple pecorino strudel, 174
bread and Pecorino soup, 64
malfattini of ricotta and rocket, 98
tagliatelle with fried egg and, 83
pennette al dolcelatte, 88
peppers: twice-roasted red peppers, 26
pesto, coriander and goat's cheese, 20
pheasant: roast breast of pheasant wrapped in smoked bacon, 120
pickle, sweet and sour grape, 188
pizzas, 90–93
polenta, soft Gorgonzola, 132
potatoes: *aligot* (cheese and potato purée), 135
goat's cheese and parsley mash, 146
goyère, 37
potato and Cantal soup, 54
potato cakes with ricotta, 145
prawns, sizzling, 112
pressed cheese with dried fruits, 183
provolone: *involtini di melanzane al formaggio*, 136
prune soufflé, hot, 173

quails stuffed with Sage Derby, 118
quark: crunchy quark pavlovas, 158
quark mayonnaise, 21
quark, prune and white chocolate tart, 163

radicchio, mushroom and chive salad, 78
ratatouille-stuffed mozzarella, 34
ravioli: Topfenravioli, 86
Reblochon baked in Savoy cabbage, 42
Red Leicester, gratin of leeks with, 131
red mullet on baked salad caprese, 101
rhubarb in chilled punch syrup, 150
rice: asparagus risotto with fonduta, 96
crispy cheese risotto *al salto*, 97

suppli alla Gorgonzola con basilico, 94
ricotta: baked amaretti peaches with, 179
    baked bucatini with garlic cheese and
        ricotta sauce, 84
    crispy cheese risotto *al salto*, 97
    grilled chicken spatchcock with, 116
    lemon blini with raspberries and, 170
    malfattini of ricotta and rocket, 98
    panna 'ri-cotta', 156
    potato cakes with chives and, 145
    ricotta, lemon thyme and garlic
        butter, 19
    Sambuca-flamed ricotta, 149
rigatoni with mixed peppers, 88
Roquefort: aubergine and Roquefort
    soufflé, 134
    flamiche aux trois fromages, 41
    grilled steak tartare with, 121
    pepper-crusted rib eye of beef with
        Roquefort butter, 122
    Roquefort and green peppercorn
        butter, 19
    Roquefort and red cabbage salad, 73
    Roquefort butter, 19
Roubiliac: goat's cheese and parsley
    mash, 146
    plum tomato salad with goat's milk
        dressing, 67
    roasted aubergine *moutabel* with, 36

saganaki, 36
Sage Derby, quails stuffed with, 118
Sainte-Maure, poached figs stuffed
    with, 160

salads, 67-81
saltimbocca, new-look, 126
Sambuca-flamed ricotta, 149
sardines, stuffed, 109
sauces, 18
sausages, herb cheese, 142
sea bass, Parmesan-crusted, 102
semi-hard cheeses, 9-10
sheep's cheeses: Greek-style baked
        artichokes, 44
    saganaki, 36
sheep's milk turnovers, Cretan, 180
shortcrust pastry, 21
skate: wing of skate with Camembert, 106
smoked cod's roe: taramasalata, 25
soft cheeses, 10-11
sorbet, cheese, 150
soufflés, 134, 173
soups, 51-65
spinach, blue cheese and avocado
    salad, 72
Stilton: pear, celeriac and Stilton
    vichyssoise, 51
    Stilton bread, 23
    summer fruit gratin with apricot Stilton
        sauce, 168
stocks, 16-17
storing cheese, 9-12
strudel, apple pecorino, 174
suppli alla Gorgonzola con basilico, 94
swede mash with Cheddar, 146

tagliatelle with fried egg, capers and
    pecorino Sardo, 83

Taleggio, Parmesan brioche toast with, 32
taramasalata on cream cheese, 25
tarts: Cashel Blue and pecan pie, 176
    flamiche aux trois fromages, 41
    goyère, 37
    quark, prune and white chocolate, 163
tomatoes: plum tomato salad, 67
    tomato gazpacho, 58
Tomme: *aligot*, 135
    grilled chicken spatchcock with, 116
Topfenravioli, 86
tourte de Poitou, 178
turbot, wine-roasted, 108
turnips stuffed with mascarpone creamed
        spinach and Beaufort cheese, 141

veal: new-look saltimbocca, 126
    steaks with blue cheese rarebit, 125
vegetables, 131-47
    roasted vegetable pizza, 91
    saffron vegetable chowder, 65
    vegetable stock, 16
    winter vegetable Pan Haggerty, 140
vichyssoise, 51
vinaigrette, goat's cheese and cumin, 20

walnut gnocchi, baked, 97
Wensleydale: spiced apple and
        Wensleydale pie, 172
wines, 13-14

yoghurt *see* labna

zuppa Pavese, 54

ACKNOWLEDGEMENTS

Although I am the author of this book, I am only one of a select team of people who
made *A Passion for Cheese* possible. My sincere thanks go to:
- Jane Middleton, for her superb editing of the manuscript: this is our second book
together and I thank her immensely
- Photographer Gus Filgate, home economist Louise Pickford and stylist Penny
Markham who, between them, creatively enliven these pages
- Michael Day and Simon Yorke of the Huge Cheese Company for their invaluable
help and for sharing their wealth of knowledge
- Fiona Lindsay and Linda Shanks, my agents, for their continued backing
- James and Cathy Lane (Gospel Green) and Kevin and Alison Blunt (Golden Cross)
for giving us the use of their farm to photograph, and to Nic Barlow for the
wonderful shots taken there
- My team of chefs here at The Lanesborough, for their help and daily devotion
to good food
- Finally, a big thank you to Kyle Cathie and Candida Hall for their hard work and
enthusiasm for *A Passion for Cheese*, from its initial concept to the finished article.